# Celebrating the Birth of CHRIST

Worship, Preaching, and
Program Resources for Christmas

**By J. Michael Shannon/Robert C. Shannon**

STANDARD PUBLISHING
Cincinnati, Ohio     3022

Sharing the thoughts of their own hearts, the authors may express views not entirely consistent with those of the publisher.

**Library of Congress Cataloging in Publication Data**

Shannon, J. Michael.
  Celebrating the birth of Christ.

  1. Christmas. 2. Worship programs. I. Shannon,
Robert, 1930-    . II. Title.
BV45.S4  1985    263'.91    84-26808
ISBN 0-87239-916-8

Cover picture © 1985, Glen Eshelman Photography.

# CONTENTS

# INTRODUCTION

To the preacher, Christmas offers the greatest opportunity of the whole year. People who rarely attend church through the year will come at Christmas. Can something be said that will bring them back? People whose hearts are hard are often softened at Christmas. Can that be used to get the gospel inside?

Christmas also offers the greatest challenge of the whole year. What can be said that has not been said a thousand times before? Perhaps nothing, but surely it can be said in a fresh way. Can the preacher tell the old, old story in ways that are new enough to be interesting and different enough to be memorable?

Yes! He can put a new robe on old and familiar truths. He can display them in a different light. He can show neglected aspects, nuances, and applications. That's what this book is all about. The message of Christmas is ageless. It cannot be changed, and it ought not be changed. But the very fact that we are so familiar with it puts special demands on the preacher. In fact, the highest challenge a preacher faces is that of saying something fresh about old and familiar texts. We have within us the conviction the divine truth is always inexhaustible. We are certain that it is possible to be original and creative in preaching the birth of our Lord. But it is not easy. It demands our very best efforts.

This opportunity and challenge come to the preacher at the most difficult time of the year. If others are busy, he is doubly busy. The pressures of time and duties are multiplied for him. That is why this book was written. For in the midst of his busiest weeks, the preacher wants very much to rise to the challenge and opportunity of preaching at Christmastime.

The material here is meant to be used either directly or indirectly. Let it be the spark that sets afire your own imagination. Let it be the catalyst that precipitates your own creative powers. Let it be the key that unlocks the potential for your own originality.

# WORSHIP RESOURCES

# CALLS TO WORSHIP

"Blessed is the man that feareth the Lord, that delighteth greatly in his commandments."

Psalm 112:1

O Lord, we seek that blessedness that comes from knowing Thee, from keeping company with Thee. We seek Thy face. O turn not from us, Father, but receive us as Thy children. In Jesus' name.

"Great is the Lord, and greatly to be praised; and his greatness is unsearchable."

Psalm 145:3

"O God, Thou art my God; I shall seek Thee earnestly; my soul thirsts for Thee, my flesh yearns for Thee. . . . Because Thy lovingkindness is better than life, my lips will praise Thee. So I will bless Thee as long as I live; I will lift up my hands in Thy name."

Psalm 63:1, 3, 4
New American Standard Bible

"And after these things I heard a great voice of much people in heaven, saying, Alleluia; Salvation, and glory, and honor, and power, unto the Lord our God."

Revelation 19:1

"Seek ye the Lord while he may be found, call ye upon him while he is near."

Isaiah 55:6

"Thou shalt worship the Lord thy God, and him only shalt thou serve."

Matthew 4:10

"O clap your hands, all ye people; shout unto God with the voice of triumph. For the Lord most high is terrible; he is a great King over all the earth."

Psalm 47:1, 2

"And every creature which is in heaven, and on the earth, and under the earth, and such as are in the sea, and all that are in them, heard I saying, Blessing, and honor, and glory, and power, be unto him that sitteth upon the throne, and unto the Lamb for ever and ever. . . . Amen."

Revelation 5:13, 14

"As the hart panteth after the water brooks, so panteth my soul after thee, O God. My soul thirsteth for God."

Psalm 42:1, 2

"Hear . . . O Lord, attend unto my cry; give ear unto my prayer."

Psalm 17:1

"Trust in the Lord with all thine heart; and lean not unto thine own understanding. In all thy ways acknowledge him, and he shall direct thy paths."

Proverbs 3:5, 6

"Unto thee, O God, do we give thanks, unto thee do we give thanks: for that thy name is near thy wondrous works declare."

Psalm 75:1

"And all the angels . . . fell before the throne on their faces, and worshipped God, saying, Amen: Blessing, and glory, and wisdom, and thanksgiving, and honor, and power, and might, be unto our God for ever and ever. Amen."

Revelation 7:11, 12

# PRAYERS

We thank Thee, O God, that in this changing world, some things endure. Above all else today, we praise Thy changeless mercy and Thy enduring grace. Accept now our grateful worship in Jesus' name. Amen.

Save us, O Lord, from the temptation to take lightly this privilege. Sanctify these moments of worship by Thy own presence. As we have set apart this hour, wilt Thou set us apart for Thyself. Remove our sins. Remember them against us no more. Then bring us, cleansed and redeemed, before Thy holy face this day. Through Christ the Savior, amen.

For Thy might and power, O God, we praise Thee—for the abundance of Thy blessings and the sweetness of Thy tender mercies. Thou hast blessed us far beyond that which we deserve. Thou has not dealt with us after our sins or remembered us according to our iniquities. Hear then, O God, our prayers this day, and accept our acts of worship. Through Jesus Christ our Lord, amen.

Remove, O Lord, the vanity that blinds us to our smallness and to Thy greatness. Give us today a glimpse of Thee upon Thy throne, and help us to see ourselves as Thou dost see us. In Jesus' name, amen.

Dear Father, grant us another kind of responsive reading. We have read together from Your Book. Now help us to respond in life, in character, and in deed. Make every moment in the new week a response to the reading of Your Word. Bless these moments spent in worship, and sanctify them with Your presence. Then sanctify us for Your service. Set us apart that we may be instruments of Your peace, Your wisdom, and Your life. Help us to avoid temptation and sin. Forgive us when we fail. Grant us at last an eternal home. Through Christ our Lord, amen.

Lord, it is more than custom that brings us here today, and more than habit that causes us to bow in prayer. How deep is our need of Thee. Thou alone canst cleanse the leper's spots. Thou alone canst comfort. Thou alone canst strengthen. Thou alone givest life.

Forgive the self-seeking that dominates our lives. Forgive the self-serving that makes us judge all things by our own self-interest. We confess that sometimes we have even been selfish in our prayers. Reach out, O God, to those who need Thee so desperately. Reach out through us to those who seek Thy help. Through our lives may men be led to the Christ in whose name we pray. Amen.

Dear Father, we come confessing that we have transgressed Thy laws and disobeyed Thy commandments. We have done what we ought not to have done and have left undone that which we ought to have done. We pray for Thy forgiveness.

Forgive Thy church, O Lord, for leaving its true mission to pursue hobbies and pastimes. Forgive our nation when our national policies are less than honest, when they lack compassion, and when they are not true to moral principle.

Bless those who are hungry that they may be fed, those who are naked that they may be clothed, and those who are friendless that they may be sensitive to Your presence. Through Christ our Lord, amen.

Forgive us, O God, if we weaken Thy power, stain Thy honor, diminish Thy glory, or make more difficult Thy salvation of lost men. We pray through Christ our Lord, amen.

Save us, O God, from that vain and empty worship that characterizes the pagan and the Pharisee. Make these moments so meaningful that all of life will be different because we have been here this day. Implant Thy Word in our minds and Thy Spirit in our hearts. We pray for the men who hold the political power of world government, for those who in war have the power to take life and devastate lands, and for those who hold in their hands the spiritual power of truth.

We pray for those weakened by sickness and disease and by the years. We pray for those weakened by temptation, doubt, and fear. Make us like Christ, in whose name we pray. Amen.

Dear Lord, we are gathered together in Thy name. We come to claim the promise, "Here am I in the midst." Humble us today with the knowledge that Thou art truly with us as we worship Thee. Through Christ our Lord, amen.

O Lord, Thou who has brought us to a new day's dawning and to a new week, create within us a new heart. Help us to put off the old man with his deeds. Make us new creatures in Christ Jesus, created unto good works. Help us to be workmanship of which Thy Son shall not be ashamed. In His dear name, amen.

O Lord, may what we hear in our ears today find lodging in our hearts so that it might find expression in our lives. For Jesus' sake, amen.

Holy is the ground on which we stand today, O Lord. We confess to You our unworthiness. We are unworthy of Your blessings; we are unworthy of Your forgiveness; we are unworthy even to come into Your presence. But we do come because You bid us come. Make us what we can be. Make us what we ought to be. Make us what we were meant to be. Through Christ our Lord, amen.

# STEWARDSHIP MEDITATIONS

Giving is as essential to our spiritual health as prayer and the reading of God's Word. It is an outlet for thanksgiving, a tangible hymn of praise, and the inevitable gesture of a loving heart.

Paul says, "If we have sown unto you spiritual things, is it a great thing if we shall reap your carnal things?" Ordinarily men sow in order to reap. Here we reap in order to sow. We reap your material things in order that the church may sow spiritual seed in this community and around the world.

"Covetousness puts money ahead of manhood. It shackles its devotee and makes him its victim. It hardens the heart and deadens the noble impulses and destroys the vital qualities of life" (H. C. Moore). Good stewardship protects us from covetousness.

Life is a trust from God. We own nothing. We are administrators of the estate God has entrusted to us. When we bring our tithes and offerings into the storehouse, we are fulfilling the responsibilities of that trusteeship that God has placed in our keeping.

"Money is a good slave but a bad master. Property belongs in the purse or the bank, but not in the heart. Wealth has its place and its power, but it is not entitled to occupy the throne or sway the scepter" (H. C. Moore). We give today to show who rules in our hearts.

Someone said there are three kinds of givers, the flint, the sponge, and the honeycomb. To get anything out of a flint, you must hammer it. To get anything out of the sponge, you must squeeze it. But the honeycomb just overflows with sweetness. Was it this last that was in mind when the Bible verse was written, "The Lord loveth a cheerful giver"?

Giving is not an interlude in the midst of worship, but an integral part of worship.

The Lord said to Moses, "Speak unto the children of Israel, that they bring me an offering: of every man that giveth it willingly with his heart ye shall take my offering."

—Exodus 25:2

# COMMUNION MEDITATIONS

Does it seem strange to talk about death on a day we associate with birth? Does it ruin the happiness and the joy? It shouldn't. After all, the angels announced to Mary and Joseph before Jesus was born that He would save His people from their sins. The only way this salvation could be accomplished was on a cross. Though we want to center our thoughts on the baby in the manger, we must recognize that He came to face the cross for us. Therefore, we should not be the least bit uncomfortable to come around His table during the Christmas season.

Though the arrival of Jesus caught the world somewhat by surprise, He was part of God's eternal plan. We mark His birth because of who He was and what He came to do. We also this day mark His death, because that was the fulfillment of His purpose. As the Christmas carol says, "Come, Desire of nations, come! Fix in us Thy humble home: Rise, the woman's conquering seed, bruise in us the serpent's head; Adam's likeness now efface, stamp thine image in its place: second Adam from above, reinstate us in thy love." This great task was accomplished not at Bethlehem, but at Calvary. And so we would remember that, too, this Christmas season.

When Jesus was presented in the temple, He was met by Simeon, a devout man who had been waiting for the Messiah. Simeon blessed the child, but added some very discouraging words. He said, "Behold, this child is set for the fall and rising again of many in Israel; and for a sign which shall be spoken against; (yea, a sword shall pierce through thy own soul, also;) that the thoughts of many hearts may be revealed." Even at this early moment, we see the destiny of Jesus. We see that He was to walk the road of suffering and death. And we also see that because of His sufferings, the thoughts of many may be revealed. That's what happened at the cross, and that's what happens as we remember the cross around the Lord's table.

16

The Christmas flower, the poinsettia, is a member of the same family as a plant called the crown of thorns. This reminds us that Christmas is related to Good Friday, that the baby Jesus became our Savior and Redeemer through His suffering on the cross. Let us not forget the crown of thorns as we gaze at the poinsettias.

Should we be surprised that the babe of Bethlehem was destined to die a death at the hands of evil men? Even in Jesus' infancy, He was considered threat enough for Herod to attempt to take His life. Herod did not succeed with his plans because it was not the right time for Jesus to face death. But later Jesus did face death for you and for me. And even for the wicked men who sent Him to the cross.

At Jesus' birth, He was surrounded by ordinary people. All His life, the ordinary people heard Him gladly. In the upper room, He was surrounded by disciples, who were ordinary people. So today as we come around His table, we recognize that it was for ordinary people that Jesus came into the world, and it was for people like us that He died. He takes the ordinary people and makes them extraordinary through the redemption He accomplished on the cross.

No one wants to be sad at Christmas. Yet every Christmas we hear of some family who has a tragedy at this time of year. Even the Christmas story has its own tragedy. We see how Herod, in his vain attempt to put Christ to death, slaughtered the innocent in Bethlehem. So we see joy mingled with sorrow. And today as we come around the table, we have joy mingled with sorrow.

Many of the Jews expected their Messiah to come with a flaming sword to battle against their foes. Instead, God came down to earth with a rattle in His hand. Still, He did come to do battle, to battle against Satan and sin.

God is always surprising us. Just as He surprised us by coming into the world as a baby, He surprised us by winning the victory through death on the cross. The victory was accomplished, and that is what we celebrate as we come around the Lord's table.

# PREACHING RESOURCES

# SERMON IDEAS

**The Born-Again Christ** (Galatians 4:19)
"O Holy Child of Bethlehem ... be born in us today."
—Phillips Brooks

**The Unbelievable Report** (Isaiah 52:13—53:1)
Too Miraculous to Accept
Too Good to Be True
Too Distant to Be Appreciated
Too Revolutionary to Be Believed

**Christmas Journeys** (Matthew 2)
A Journey of Discovery (Matthew 2:1, 2)
A Journey of Necessity (Matthew 2:12)
A Journey of Escape (Matthew 2:13)
A Journey of Violence (Matthew 2:16)

**Behold, the Arm of the Lord** (Isaiah 52:9, 10; 53:1)
His Gracious Arm Reaching Down
His Powerful Arm Reaching Out
His Loving Arm Embracing

**Going Home for Christmas** (Matthew 2:13)
An Unfamiliar Way
A Less Convenient Way
A More Costly Way
A More Dangerous Way
A Less Traveled Way

**Christmas People** (Titus 2:11-15)
Christ Makes Us ...
Righteous People
Hopeful People
Redeemed People
Consecrated People

21

**The Gift of Life** (John 1:4)
    An Endless Life
    A Sinless Life
    A Selfless Life

**What Do You Want for Christmas**
    A Sense of Worth
    A Sense of Peace
    A Sense of Forgiveness

**The God Who Loved—And Gave** (John 3:16)
    The Breadth of His Love: the World
    The Depth of His Love: He Gave His Son
    The Length of His Love: Everlasting

**For Unto You Is Born ...** (Luke 2:11)
    The Savior: the Redemption of Jesus
    The Christ: the Nature of Jesus
    The Lord: the Authority of Jesus

**The God Who Plans Ahead** (Galatians 4:4, 5)
    The Timing of His Coming
    The Manner of His Coming
    The Purpose of His Coming

**The Bread of Heaven** (John 6:47-51)
    The world hungered for God.
    God answered that need in Christ, the Bread of life.
    The need can only be met if people partake of the Bread.

**The Day After Christmas** (Luke 2:17-20)
    Christmas inspires witness.
    Christmas inspires joy.
    Christmas inspires praise.
    Christmas inspires change.

# SERMON OUTLINES

## WHEN THEY SAW THE STAR
Matthew 2:10

The brightest star in our sky is a man-made star.

I. IT CONFIRMED THE PROMISE.
   A. They journeyed by faith.
   B. We must journey by faith.
   C. Those who launch out on faith deserve confirmation.
      1. For them it was the star.
      2. We see God's promise confirmed in nature, human nature, history, and experience.

II. IT POINTED THE WAY.
   A. Sometimes the most difficult part of a journey is in the last few miles.
   B. The star pointed the way for them.
   C. Spiritually speaking, the star points the way for all mankind.

III. IT IDENTIFIED THE CHRIST.
   A. The focus of their worship was the Person, not the star.
   B. Our worship is never to be directed toward things, but toward the Creator of all things.
   C. We do not worship objects, like the sacred stone of Islam.
   D. Many things help identify Christ for us.

The value of Christmas is that it clears our eyes so that we may see the star, and following it, find the Savior.

# THE CHRISTMAS LIGHTS
Isaiah 9:2

Help! Cried the baby bat in fright!
Turn on the dark;
I'm afraid of the light.
                    —Silverstein

I. THE GREAT DARKNESS
   A. The darkness of sin
   B. The darkness of human failure
   C. The darkness of death

II. THE GREAT LIGHT
   A. The light of a personal Savior
   B. The light of an endless joy
   C. The light of an eternal life

III. THE LESSER LIGHTS
   A. Men are like candles: some are cold and never lit; some
      are twisted and melted but have felt the flame; some
      have burned down to the socket!
   B. "Lives of great men all remind us we may make our
      lives sublime."
   C. Christmas is the time to consider our example.
   D. Do we spread spiritual light or spiritual darkness in the
      world?

A boy was in St. Paul's Cathedral in London, standing before
Holman Hunt's famous painting of Jesus as the light of the
world. You've seen reproductions of it: Jesus is standing at the
door, knocking. Finally the boy spoke: "Did He ever get in?"

# I'LL BE GLAD WHEN IT'S OVER
Luke 2:10, 11

You hear that all the time in the weeks before Christmas. "I'll be glad when it's over."

I. IT SHOWS US THE DISTRACTIONS OF CHRISTMAS.
   A. The devil has diverted us from Christmas, not by denying it so much as by covering it up with tinsel and trappings.
   B. We are distracted by money to be spent or money to be earned.
   C. We are distracted by pleasure.
   D. We are even distracted by family.

II. IT SHOWS US THE DISTORTIONS OF CHRISTMAS.
   A. Receiving, not giving
   B. Exchanging, not giving
   C. Playing, not praying
   D. Holiday, not holy day

III. IT SHOWS US THE FORGOTTEN DIMENSIONS OF CHRISTMAS
   A. It really is a time for receiving—for receiving spiritual gifts of grace and peace.
   B. It really is a time for exchanging—for exchanging our faith and loyalty for His forgiveness and love.
   C. It really is a time for pleasure—not the physical pleasures of food and drink and romance, but the spiritual pleasures of prayer and worship and thanksgiving.

The food will run out, the tree will dry out, the candles will burn out, the presents will wear out, the lights will fade out, and the money will run out. Then, if we look back, perhaps we can see the real Christmas.

# THE ROAD TO BETHLEHEM

No longer Caesar's legions tramp the roads to Rome.
No more to Tyre or Babylon, proud kings come riding home.
The routes to Nineveh are dark. No couriers travel them.
Still the heart—star led—shall find the road to Bethlehem.

—Chesterton

I. SOME CAME WITH HASTE (Luke 2:10).
   A. The shepherds hurried along the road.
   B. Contrast that with our Christmas rush!
      1. Theirs was the haste of excitement, enthusiasm, faith, commitment.
      2. They hurried to get *to* Christmas.
      3. We hurry to get *through* Christmas.

II. SOME CAME WITH JOY (Luke 2:10).
   A. Joy because God's Word was true
   B. Joy because God's promise was fulfilled
   C. Joy because the King had come

III. SOME CAME WITH VIOLENCE (Matthew 2:16).
   A. It seems a shame—blood splattered on this lovely story.
   B. Jesus came into a real world.
   C. Violence seems worse at Christmastime.

IV. SOME CAME WITH DEVOTION (Matthew 2:2).
   A. Worship was so important to them that they made a long journey.
   B. How important is worship to you?
   C. If worship is not as important as it ought to be, perhaps you need to understand the *true identity* of the One we worship.

For some, the journey is short. For some, it is long. But all must travel the Bethlehem road.

# THE THREE KINGS OF CHRISTMAS

I refer not to the Wise-men. ("We Three Kings of Orient are; bearing gifts, we traverse afar!")

I. THE KING OF PEACE (Augustus Caesar)
   A. John begins his Gospel in Heaven, Matthew in Eden, Luke in Rome.
   B. Caesar called himself savior and son of God; and he brought peace to the world.
   C. He moved men like pawns on a chessboard.
   D. Yet within three centuries, Rome would belong not to Caesar, but to Christ.

II. THE KING OF VIOLENCE (Herod)
   A. He was only a puppet king.
   B. Everybody understood he was a puppet of the emperor. We know he was a puppet of the devil.
   C. He killed his own sons. He did not hesitate to kill the sons at Bethlehem. If he could, he would have killed the Son of God.
   D. Ironically, his burial place is within sight of Jesus' birthplace. Thousands go to Bethlehem, only a few to the Herodium!

III. THE KING OF KINGS (Jesus)
   A. The simple came. Those shepherds were not necessarily ignorant, but they were simple, uncomplicated, unsophisticated men. How often does sophistication and culture keep people from Christ?
   B. The strangers came—the Wise-men. (What strange people Christianity attracts, and always has!)
   C. Perhaps there were others who visited the infant Christ, but whose visits are not recorded. These show two extremes: educated and uneducated; powerful and lowly; wealthy and poor; expected and unexpected.

Will you cast your lot with political power (Caesar), with force (Herod), or with love and peace (Jesus)?

# LISTEN, GOD IS SPEAKING
## Hebrews 1:1-3

The author of Hebrews says that God spoke to us in His Son.

I. HOW DID HE SPEAK?
   A. Gently
   B. Clearly
   C. Lovingly
   D. Finally
   E. Commandingly

II. WHAT DID HE SAY?
   A. "I Care."
   B. "I can make you better than you are."
   C. "I can forgive your sins."
   D. "I can give you life eternal."
   E. "I love you."

Jesus is God's beloved son. Hear ye Him.


# SURPRISE
## Luke 2:8-14

God delights in surprising us. No event was more surprising than Jesus' birth.

I. SUDDENLY—A SONG
   A. A song of praise
   B. A song of hope
   C. A song of peace
   D. A song of love

II. SUDDENLY—A SON
   A. He will reveal the Father's nature.
   B. He will bear the Father's message.
   C. He will do the Father's will.

III. SUDDENLY—A SAVIOR
   A. He saves us from our empty religion.
   B. He saves us from ourselves.
   C. He saves us from our sins.

So sing the song, know the Son, and let the Savior do His work in you.

# THE *NIGHT* BEFORE CHRISTMAS
### Matthew 4:16

The familiar poem highlights for us a lesser-known truth. In many ways, it was *night* before Christmas.

I. WE WERE IN THE DARK ABOUT MAN.
   A. About his potential
   B. About his destiny

II. WE WERE IN THE DARK ABOUT SIN.
   A. Sin made His coming to earth necessary.
   B. Sin tried to frustrate Him at every turn.
   C. Finally sin tried to kill Him.
   D. Theft and violence are more common at Christmas and touch us more deeply.

III. WE WERE IN THE DARK ABOUT GOD.
   A. Christmas confirms His love for us.
   B. Christmas confirms His grace.
   C. Christmas confirms His power.
   D. Christmas confirms His judgment.

These are the true Christmas lights, not the twinkling colored bulbs, but these shining truths.


# SPECIAL REPORT
### Luke 2:8-14

When we see the words "Special Report" or "News Bulletin," we listen attentively because we know something of great importance has happened. No special report was more dramatic than the one delivered to the shepherds.

I. IT WAS SURPRISING NEWS.
II. IT WAS JOYOUS NEWS.
III. IT WAS UNIVERSAL NEWS.
IV. IT WAS PERSONAL NEWS.
V. IT WAS LIFE-CHANGING NEWS.
VI. IT WAS MUCH-NEEDED NEWS.

Only a few times in our lives will we hear news that will dramatically change the way we live. This is the greatest event in world history. You must tell it, and respond to it.

# LET US GO ... AND SEE

## Luke 2:15

The immediate response of the shepherds to the angels' message was "Let's go ... and see this thing which has come to pass." What did they see?

I. A HUMBLE BIRTH
   A. Humble parents
   B. Humble town
   C. Humble surroundings

II. A HUMAN BIRTH
   A. He came into the world in human form
   B. He came to address the human condition
   C. He came to share human problems
   D. He came to show the human potential

III. A HOLY BIRTH
   A. Foretold by prophets
   B. Announced by angels
   C. Prepared by the Father

Won't you go with the shepherds to see this birth? If you do, you, too, will leave rejoicing.


# THE CHRISTMAS TREE

Some say the first Christmas tree in America was in 1847 in Wooster, Ohio; some in Reading, Pennsylvania, in 1804. Americans use 35,000,000 Christmas trees each year. There is also a Christmas tree in the Bible.

I. THE FAMILY TREE (Luke 3:23 ff)
   A. Identified Him with us
   B. Identified Him with prophecy
   C. Identified Him with sin and sinners

II. THE CROSS TREE (Luke 2:10, 11)
   A. Simeon saw it (Luke 2:34, 35).
   B. Isaiah saw it (Isaiah 53:4-6, 9-12).
   C. The Psalmist saw it (Psalm 22:1, 7-9, 14-18; Psalm 22:1).

III. THE LARGER TREE
   The cross is superior to the cradle for these reasons:
   A. It shows God's love more clearly.
   B. It shows sin more starkly.
   C. It shows grace more convincingly.

Every time you see one of those modern trees, think of these Biblical Christmas trees.

# SOMETHING SPECIAL
Matthew 1:1-25; Luke 1:26-38

Everyone agrees that Christmas is a special time. What makes it special is the extraordinary one who came down to us. Everything about Him and His birth is special.

I. BORN INTO A SPECIAL FAMILY (Matthew 1:1-17)
   A. A descendant of Abraham
   B. A descendant of David
   C. A descendant of sinners
   D. A descendant of Gentiles

II. BORN TO SPECIAL PARENTS
   A. Joseph (Matthew 1:18-25)
      1. A righteous man
      2. A compassionate man
   B. Mary (Luke 1:28, 38)
      1. A virtuous woman
      2. A committed woman

III. BORN IN A SPECIAL WAY (Matthew 1:18; Luke 1:35)
   A. By a biological miracle
   B. By a spiritual miracle

IV. BORN FOR A SPECIAL PURPOSE
   A. To set up an eternal kingdom (Luke 1:31-33)
   B. To save people from their sins (Matthew 1:21)

Why not let God's special Son do His special work in you?

# ILLUSTRATIONS

Jews observe Hanukkah about the same time that Christians celebrate Christmas. Hanukkah recalls the events of 164 B.C. when Judas Maccabeus reclaimed power and purged and restored the temple at Jerusalem after years of uselessness. On the day of dedication, there was only enough oil for the temple lamps to burn for one day. According to Jewish tradition, the lamps continued to burn, miraculously, for eight days. Of course there is nothing in the Bible about this, and it is likely such a miracle never occurred. But this is the background for Hanukkah and the motto of Hanukkah is, "A Great Miracle Has Happened!" What a pitiful contrast to the great miracle of Christmas. We commemorate a greater event, a greater miracle, a better light.

In Iceland there are places where fiery volcanic activity goes on under the glacier! Even so, beneath the icy exterior of some lives, there still smolders spiritual desire! At Christmas, it breaks out!

One Christmas Sunday, a minister preached on the subject of Franklin D. Roosevelt. James T. Cleland remarked that that was not totally inappropriate, since Christmas is God's "New Deal"!

A man said that in his childhood, they were so poor his mother could only afford one piece of candy at Christmas. She melted it in hot water and each child took a leaf. She put one drop of the liquid on each leaf, and the children licked them.

He kept the leaf and put it out every Christmas. When one visitor asked about it, he said, "That's the Christmas leaf. Every year I take it out and lick it, and I remember how sweet Christmas was then!"

Her husband had just died, and it didn't seem fitting to put up Christmas decorations. But she decided to put up just one—a nativity scene. She said, "I didn't put it up because my husband died, but because Jesus was born."

In an affluent neighborhood in California, a family decided to go out on Christmas Eve and serenade their neighbors with carols. In one house where they stopped, there was hectic confusion with Christmas preparations and with rushing and tension; so the lady opened the door and said to the singers, "Not now, please; we're too busy." The gentleman in the group merely said, "Yes, ma'am," and they moved away. It was Bing and Kathy Crosby with their family. If Jesus comes to our house and we say, "Not now, I'm busy," He'll move away, too.

When we give each other Christmas presents in His name, let us remember that He has given us the sun, the moon, the stars, the earth with its forests, oceans, and mountains, and everything that lives and moves. He has given us all great things and everything that blossoms and bears fruit—and all that we quarrel about and everything that we have misused. And to save us from all our selfishness and foolishness and from all our sins, He came down to earth and gave us himself.

We imagine the Bible lands on such a grand scale, it's hard for us to conceive of the fact that the site of Jesus' birth in Bethlehem and the site of His death on Golgatha are only about ten miles apart. The proximity of the places of His birth and death remind us of the fact that Jesus came into the world to die for sinners.

In the famous musical Mame, there is a production number that continually repeats the refrain, "We need a little Christmas right this very minute." Many people feel that way. The Christmas holiday inspires them and makes them ready for the new year. But the Christian can have a Christmas whenever he needs it, for Christ is constantly present.

People were amazed a few years ago when then Chicago mayor Jane Byrne announced that she and her husband were moving from their posh apartment to live in a high rise in the infamous housing project called "Cabrini Green." Cabrini Green was noted for drug trafficking, prostitution, murders, gang warfare, and loan sharking. But the mayor's move was not nearly as dramatic as the move God made. God came down to our crime-infested planet in the person of Jesus Christ. He surrendered His glory to mix with the grime and grit of life on earth.

The birth of a baby meant new life to Jennifer Forsthoffer. The newspapers carried the story of how Bill and Doris Forsthoffer could only do one thing to save the life of their daughter, who was dying of leukemia. The only thing they could do was to have another child whose bone marrow could be implanted into Jennifer's. In a very real sense, the birth of a baby brought new life to Jennifer. We can't help but be reminded that the birth of a baby, Jesus, means new life for all of us.

In C. S. Lewis' book *The Lion, The Witch and the Wardrobe*, he takes us to the land of Narnia. When Narnia is living under the authority of the witch, it is "always winter, but never Christmas." Can you imagine how discouraging that would be to a child? Still, there are people today who are living in a winter, and Christmas never comes to them. What joy could be theirs if only they would allow Christmas to come to their hearts!

A submarine was disabled beneath the sea along the Massachusetts coast. Rescue operations were begun at once. Divers communicated with those inside by tapping on the hull in Morse code. Time was running out. From inside a question was slowly tapped, "Is there any hope?" They were finally rescued, but if you listen, you can still hear that tapping. "Is there any hope?" Christmas answers, "Yes!" It is an emphatic "Yes!" It is a joyful "Yes!" It is a glorious "Yes!"

Bethlehem's Church of the Nativity was first built by St. Helen in 325. Destroyed in 529, it was rebuilt thereafter. The Persians did not destroy it because the mosaic on the wall pictured Christ's birth—and the Wise-men were Persians! The Muslims later came, but they venerate Jesus as a prophet; so they did not destroy it. Today, it is the oldest church building in the world. It is fascinating to think that the Wise-men who protected Jesus from Herod protected the church that honors His birth as well.

The first voice broadcast on radio was a religious broadcast. In 1906, a program of Christmas music was broadcast to ships at sea. Surely, this seemed almost as dramatic to those sailors as the angel's message was to the Galilean shepherds.

One prophecy about Christ's coming says that "every valley shall be exalted, and every mountain and hill shall be made low." Another says, "A highway shall there be." Rocks impede travel, but we grind them up and make a smooth road to speed travel. The ancient tar pits held primitive animals fast, but we melt the tar and smooth our roads. All those things that once hindered travel now accelerate it. So Christ took the obstacles of life and made them paving stones on the way to Heaven. He took the stumbling blocks and made them stepping stones.

"Thou shalt call his name Jesus: for He shall save His people from their sins." That was the announcement of His birth, and forgiveness is, therefore, always at the heart of the gospel. When translators tried to find a term for forgiveness in one African language, they finally put, "God spit on the ground in front of us." In that culture, to show love, you would spit on a man's head. If two people had a disagreement, went to court, and were finally reconciled, they marked it by spitting on the ground. So Jesus reconciled us to God, and to them that meant, "God spit on the ground in front of us." Whether our description of it be crude or cultured, familiar or strange, we must all experience that reconciliation, which was the very purpose of Christ's coming into the world.

A man from America visited Budapest, Hungary. Over one building he saw a neon star. Naively he thought, "Somebody forgot to take down the Christmas decorations." Then he remembered that it was the Red Star of communism, not the star of Bethlehem! Today many are deciding whether they will follow the Red Star or the Bethlehem Star!

You can see him still, in the Middle East and in Turkey and in Greece: the shepherd, leaning on his staff, roughly dressed. It must be the most boring job on earth. When you see one sheep eat grass, you've seen them all. Among the Jews, the shepherd was looked down upon because his work prevented him from following the ritual washings they thought so important.

So from every standpoint, the shepherd was the least likely person to receive the announcement of the birth of our Lord. From every standpoint except one. From the heavenly standpoint, they were the most appropriate ones to receive the news of Christ's birth. For the One coming into the world was the *Great* Shepherd, the *Good* Shepherd who would lay down His life for His sheep.

One listens to a cricket singing in his field and considers that he has no knowledge of other crickets in other fields, some far away, some nearby. He has no knowledge even of the cricket in the field across the road. His world is one patch of weeds, and his lifetime, a single summer.

One thinks of ancient man, with no knowledge of countries and continents across the seas. His own little community is his world. He knows no other.

One thinks of the worlds unknown to us, of the outer limits of the universe about which we know next to nothing. This little ball of mud, our whole universe, and our whole lifetime, these few years. God has kept some greater knowledge in reserve for us for the future.

But once in a while, God opens a window in that larger eternal, heavenly world. He opened such a window at Bethlehem when angels appeared to shepherds. We learn this much: it is a world of heavenly messengers who do God's bidding, a world of peace, and a world where all glory is given to God.

Richard Eder, writing in the *International Herald Tribune*, makes this fascinating statement. "Truth burns all ways at once, and in a sense, it doesn't matter where you stand." Jesus came to be the living truth of God. "I am truth," He said to Pilate. "I am the way, the truth, and the life," He said to the disciples. That living truth first dawned upon the world in the events of Bethlehem. Right away, that truth began to burn its way into men's hearts: into the hearts of shepherds and Wisemen, Mary and Joseph, Anna and Simeon. It still burns its way into the hearts of men.

"Oh holy Child of Bethlehem,
Descend to us we pray.
Cast out our sin, and enter in;
Be born in us today."

The oldest book in the Bible is a book of drama: the book of Job. The newest book in the Bible is a book of drama: the book of Revelation. It is neither a timetable nor a calendar, it is a drama. And the heart of the Bible is a drama, a real-life drama. Nothing more dramatic than the birth of Christ ever happened. Nothing more dramatic has ever been alleged to have happened! It was really acted out on that little Middle Eastern stage long ago. The drama is revived in our hearts each Christmas season. It has all the elements of drama: conflict, good, evil, romance, danger, adventure, death, and rescue. It is surely the most dramatic event imaginable—and it is true!

To a Moslem, there is great merit in a visit to Mecca, and Moslems try to go at least once. It used to be thought that there was great merit in a trip to Rome, though St. David's Cathedral in Wales was so highly honored that two visits there were said to be equal to one visit to Rome. Some still believe that there is some spiritual merit in a trip to the Holy Land: to Jerusalem and Bethlehem. But we need not actually go to a physical Bethlehem. We can go in our minds. We can go in our hearts. We can heed that call, "O come, all ye faithful, . . . O come ye to Bethlehem. Come and behold Him, born the King of angels." In that spiritual journey, there is always great merit.

The largest singly-owned cattle ranch in the world is in Hawaii on the Big Island. It is the Parker Ranch and comprises 250,000 acres. It all began with John Parker, a seaman who jumped ship there in 1809. He rounded up some cattle that had been brought to the island and then allowed to run wild. From this meager beginning, there came the largest individually owned cattle ranch in the world. That is the kind of story we love: rags to riches; log cabin to White House. Of course, the gospel story is just the opposite of that: riches to rags; White House to log cabin. Paul reminds us in 2 Corinthians that "though he was rich, yet for your sakes he became poor." A close reading of the Christmas story will tell you how very poor He became. He did it so that you might be rich: rich in another kind of wealth, in the coin of another realm.

In Central Europe, they cut limbs from flowering trees in September. Then in December, those limbs are brought into the house, where the warmth forces them to blossom and their pink and white flowers usher in the Christmas season. But wherever one lives, Christmas is a time of spiritual beauty. It need not be forced or contrived. It is always there: the beauty of love, the beauty of sharing, the beauty of forgiveness. These spiritual flowers blossom at Christmas in every climate.

We cannot gaze long at the transfigured Christ;
the shining glory hurts our eyes.

We cannot gaze long at the scarlet-robed Christ;
the mockery angers and infuriates us.

We cannot gaze long at the crucified Christ;
His pain and shame grieve us.

We cannot gaze long at the towel-robed Christ
washing feet in the upper room;
His humble service embarrasses us.

That's why we love Christmas; we can gaze as long as
we like at the infant Christ.

Donald G. Barnhouse was invited to preach in a university chapel one Christmas. Walking across the campus, a professor asked him, "Are you going to preach that old farce again?" To some, Christmas is an idle tale, a fiction, a farce! To some, it is a force!

## THE MIRACLE OF DREAMS

That night when shepherds heard the song
  Of hosts angelic choiring near,
A deaf man lay in slumber's spell
  And dreamed that he could hear.

That night when in the cattle's stall
  Slept Child and mother in humble fold,
A cripple turned his twisted limbs
  And dreamed that he was whole.

That night when o'er the newborn Babe
  A tender mother rose to lean,
A loathsome leper smiled in sleep
  And dreamed that he was clean.

That night when to the mother's breast
  The little king was held secure,
A harlot slept a happy sleep
  And dreamed that she was pure.

That night when in a manger lay
  The Holy One who came to save,
A man turned in the sleep of death
  And dreamed there was no grave.
                    —Author Unknown

Cynthia Jelkman celebrates two birthdays every year. January 7 marks her entry into the world, and December 26 marks the day she received a new heart. Christmas in 1977 could have been Cynthia's last. She had a serious enlargement of the heart. Unless she had a transplant, her doctors believed she would die. After endless tests, she got the Christmas present of a lifetime. A new heart. A new chance on life. The Christmas season means to all of us a new chance for life.

39

Let not our hearts be busy inns, that have no room for Thee,
But cradles for the living Christ and His nativity.
Still driven by a thousand cares, the pilgrims come and go;
The hurried caravans press on; the inns are crowded so!
Here are the rich and busy ones, with things that must be sold,
No room for simple things within this hostelry of gold.
Yet hunger dwells within these walls, these shining walls and
　　bright,
And blindness groping here and there without a ray of light.
Oh, lest we starve, and lest we die, in our stupidity,
Come, Holy Child, within and share our hospitality.
Let not our hearts be busy inns, that have no room for Thee,
But cradles for the living Christ and His nativity.
　　　　　　　　　　　　　　　—Ralph Spaulding Cushman


It was in the middle of January when a man sitting in his living room heard a thin, piping voice singing, "O Come All Ye Faithful." He went to his front door and opened it, and there was a little boy singing Christmas carols.

He said to the boy, "What are you doing?"

The child replied, "I'm singing Christmas carols."

The man said, "Why, Son, it's the middle of January."

The little boy said, "I know, but I had the measles during Christmas, and I'm just now getting around to doing my caroling."

Nothing could get in the way of his celebration, and it really didn't matter what time of year it was. Christmas brought joy to this boy's heart, and it ought to bring joy to ours as well.


There is a legend that says that there was a little brown bird that had built its nest in the very cave in Bethlehem where Jesus Christ was born. According to the legend, the bird had never sung before; but that night, hearing the angel's song, the bird learned to sing. Ever afterwards when darkness fell, people listened to the nightingale's song, never knowing that, in fact, what they were hearing was an imitation of the angel's song. Now, of course, that is only legend. But there is truth in it; for you and I learned to sing at Bethlehem. Before Christ was born, we had nothing to sing about.

In the famous cartoon *The Family Circus*, the little boy in the family was sending a Christmas card to his grandmother. He said, "I know Grandmother likes only religious cards, so I'm sending her this one with St. Nick on it." Many of us laugh at that, but in a practical sense, we are the same as that little boy. For we take great pains to celebrate the secular Christmas, but spend little time preparing for the spiritual Christmas.

In Bud Blake's *Tiger* comic strip, two little boys were talking about Christmas. One said, "We got an artificial tree this year."
The other said, "Doesn't that bother you?"
He said, "No, not as long as the presents are real."
Though we should not be too concerned about the material aspects of Christmas, we do want to make sure that our Christmas is real.

In the *Peanuts* comic strip, one of the little girls was saying that Christmas is a time for kindness and joy, and a time when we forgive one another. Charlie Brown responds by saying, "Why just at Christmas? Why can't we be kind and forgiving all through the year?"
She looks at Charlie Brown and says, "What are you, some kind of religious fanatic?"
Wouldn't it be great if the lessons we learned at Christmas and the attitudes we consider appropriate at Christmas could be exercised the year round? Wouldn't it be great if we would risk being called religious fanatics for that purpose?

The craftsmen in Germany are known to make beautiful manger scenes. These scenes, lovingly carved out of wood, have been sold to many tourists. It is interesting to note that most of them clothe the participants in Bavarian costumes of Europe rather than the costumes that would have been worn in Jesus' day. In a sense, this is understandable. All of us should think of the Christmas story as our story. Though Jesus was born in Bethlehem, He was born for all of us. We need to view ourselves as participants, and we need to view Christ as one who makes a difference in our own age.

Kierkegaard told a parable about a prince who fell in love with a peasant maid. He had noticed her passing by on the street and was instantly infatuated. He knew that if he went to her as the prince and told of his love, she would certainly accept. That would be the loyal thing to do. But he wanted her to have a genuine love for him.

So he abandoned all of his royal finery and came to live as a peasant in her community. He shared her life with her, and in that sharing, she fell in love with him. When he came to be a part of her world, she developed a deep and abiding love.

It is because of Christ that we are able to love God. Since God, in Christ, came to be a part of our world, we are enabled to know God as He really is, and to love Him with all of our hearts.

On Christmas Eve, 1909, a young Japanese seminary student decided to change his part of the world. He moved into a small house in the worst section of Kobe, Japan. He decided that he would practice what he preached. He thought people would believe his Christian preaching if he would identify with their suffering. So it was that Toyohiko Kagawa began a life-long effort to alleviate the suffering of others. Isn't it appropriate that he made that move on Christmas Eve? For someone else made a similar decision once. God decided to move into our world and to alleviate our suffering. Christ came and sacrificed His life to make our lives better.

In Doctor Suess' wonderful children's book, *How the Grinch Stole Christmas*, we find how the Grinch mistakenly believes that he can ruin everyone's Christmas holiday by stealing their presents. On Christmas morning, expecting to hear moans and cries, the Grinch is surprised to hear carols and songs and happiness. He discovers that he has not stolen Christmas at all.

If the Grinch were to steal our presents this Christmas, would our story turn out as Dr. Suess' story? Have we become so materialistic that the Grinch could steal our Christmas? If so, then we certainly need to re-evaluate how we celebrate Christmas. For no one can rob us of the joy that Jesus Christ brought into the world.

A sign over the liquor store said, "Come here for your Christmas spirits." That message certainly illustrates the sadness of some people's celebration. If they think they can receive the Christmas spirit out of a bottle, they are certainly mistaken. Isn't it indeed sad that our Savior's birth is often marked by drunkenness and licentiousness?

A family was driving by the church a few days after Christmas when the little boy noticed that the nativity scene had been taken down. He said, innocently enough, "I see they've put Jesus away for another year." Now we all know what he meant, but there is truth in the fact that many people put Jesus away after Christmas; never knowing that His can be a constant presence the year round.

John Jacob Niles, the famous folk song authority, tells about a time many years ago when a small group of traveling evangelists came and set up their tents on the courthouse square in his town. They hung their wash on the Confederate monument. They began to preach on the courthouse square until the county commissioner decided that it was inappropriate and required them to pack up and leave. But before they left, John Jacob Niles was in the audience when a thin, pale girl, the daughter of an itinerate evangelist, got up and sang a song that he had never heard before. "I wonder as I wander out under the sky, why Jesus our Savior did come forth to die for poor, lonely people like you and like I. I wonder as I wander out under the sky."

Since he was a collector of folk songs, Niles went to her and said, "Where did you hear that song?"

She said, "I don't remember. I don't know where I learned it."

He said, "Is there more to it?"

She said, "No, I only know this one verse."

So John Jacob Niles took that song, elaborated on it, and published it. In its simplicity, it illustrates the feelings all of us surely have at Christmas. Truly we can all say, "I wonder as I wander out under the sky, why Jesus our Savior did come forth to die."

There is a story that's told of a small church that was getting ready for its annual Christmas play. The boy who was going to play the part of Joseph fell sick and had to call in at the last minute to say that he would not be available for the play. Someone asked the director of the play what they were going to do now that the actor that was going to play Joseph was sick. She said, "Well, the only thing I know to do is just write him out of the script." Unfortunately, in the world, that's what people have done with Christ. They celebrate the holiday, but they have written Jesus out of the script.

In the Frank Capra movie *It's a Wonderful Life*, the main character, George Bailey, is facing a very dismal Christmas. His business has failed because of the deceitfulness of one of the town's most influential citizens. George, believing he is ruined, determines to take his own life. He is prevented from suicide by an angel, who gives George a chance to see what life would have been like if he had never been born. George's hope is restored as he finds out that his acts of kindness have made a difference. He determines to go back into the real world and face with courage and hope whatever problems he has. Christmas is a time for us to think about the difference one person made in our lives. Consider for a moment what this world would have been like if Jesus had not come. Since He did come, can't we face life courageously and hopefully?

In the popular *Hi and Lois* comic strip, the writer often puts into words what is in the mind of the little baby girl who is the pride of the family. During a comic strip that appeared during the Christmas season, the little girl is pictured as thinking, "I sure do love Christmas, boy do I love Christmas. I don't know what it's all about yet, but I sure do love it." Many are in the same boat as this little girl. They enjoy Christmas, but they just don't know what it's all about. Think how much more enjoyment they would receive if they understood the full significance of Christmas!

At Christmas time the families sit down
   and eat at a festive table;
They sing and tell stories well into the night
   And go on for as long as they are able;
They finish the last of the pumpkin pie
   And the turkey's been stripped to the bone,
But one lonely man eats beans from a can
   And celebrates Christmas alone.

A tattered old wreath that belongs in the trash,
   Hangs from his unpainted door;
Inside his heart there are carols and songs,
   There is laughter and music galore;
He does not regret his lone celebration,
   He thinks his life's full to the brim;
For his tender heart knows and his countenance shows
   That Christ came for people like him.

The great scholar Jerome needed inspiration as he worked on translating the Scriptures. He decided that he would do his work in the cave where it is believed Jesus was born. He spent years there slaving over the Scriptures. He believed that that place would provide him the encouragement that he needed. While a visit to Bethlehem is always moving, we should all realize that Christ is constantly present. He is an ever-present help.

A tour group visiting the Holy Land was entering the groto where Jesus is believed to have been born. In the distance, they heard a very familiar tune with very unfamiliar words. It was a Christmas carol sung by a tour group of Christians from another country and with a different skin color. Though their cultures differed and their experiences varied widely, these two tour groups both worshiped the same Savior and shared the same joy while pondering the meaning of His birth.

Each year we watch the news as people gather in Bethlehem to mark Christmas in the place where Jesus was born. We watch as armed soldiers mingle with the crowd outside the church. We see body searches, metal detectors, and security booths. Fortunately, no major incidents have marred the Christmas celebrations during the last several years, although several attempts have been foiled. Isn't it a shame that the main concern in Bethlehem on Christmas is that there might be acts of violence on the night they honor the birth of Christ and in the place they believe the Prince of Peace was born?

# COMPLETE SERMONS

## ALWAYS A CHRISTMAS
John 1:5

I heard the bells on Christmas Day
Their old familiar carols play,
And wild and sweet
The words repeat,
Of peace on earth, good will to men!

And in despair I bowed my head;
"There is no peace on earth," I said.
"For hate is strong
And mocks the song
Of peace on earth, good will to men!"

Some years Christmas seems out of place. This is such a year. Nations are looking down their respective gun barrels at one another. The whole world is a lighted firecracker we are holding in our hands, wondering when it will go off. The jingle bells sound like funeral bells, tolling the knell of our dead hopes.

For some personally, Christmas seems out of place. Death, or illness, or some tragic turn of events has robbed them of the joy of Christmas. They feel like taking the wreath from the door and pinning it to the grave of their hopes. An Iowa minister was asked to write a Christmas sermon for his church's periodical. Just before he sat down to write it, his wife died. He said he was forced to view Christmas in a new and different light.

I hear two voices today: the voice of angels and the voice of anguish. The angels cry, "Glory to God in the highest." The voice of anguish is that of Rachel weeping for her children. Rachel died in childbirth and was buried at Bethlehem. So when the Babylonians began oppressing the children of Israel, the prophet Jeremiah thought he could see Rachel coming up from the grave weeping. When Herod slew the infants at

47

Bethlehem, the gospel writer thought he could hear that voice again—Rachel weeping for her children. Sometimes the voice of anguish drowns out the voice of angels.

Is there really any reason to believe that God "rules the world with truth and grace"? Doesn't Christmas belong to children, to a world we've outgrown? In a world infinitely large, can we still turn to a tiny village for our faith? In a world infinitely old, can we still believe the birth of a baby is the watershed of history? In a closed world of cause and effect, can we still believe that God entered history?

Our text assures us that we can. It is John 1:5: "The light shines in the darkness and the darkness has never put it out." There will always be a Christmas. The light is better seen in the dark. Were I to light a candle here today, it would not attract much attention. It would have to compete with the electric lights and with the sunlight coming through the windows. Should we come back tonight at midnight and light the same candle, its beams would reach the farthest and darkest corners.

Not only is it true that we keep Christmas today in an incompatible world. Christ came to an inhospitable empire. "It came to pass in those days. . . ." What were those days like? Who was Caesar Augustus? Augustus had waded to his throne through a sea of blood. Three men shared the throne—and agreed to murder 300 senators and 2,000 knights to consolidate their position. Then two of the three were eliminated, and one man alone reigned. He changed his name to Augustus, "Majestic." He declared that he was God. This is the man whose long arm reached across the Great Sea and touched a carpenter at Nazareth and forced him and his wife to go to Bethlehem for the census. Over against Christ's manger we must see Caesar's throne. How great the power that baby challenged! Then Rome was a large place and Bethlehem small. Rome made the headlines while Bethlehem could not make the back page. Today that's reversed. Why? Because of the invincible Christ.

A cartoon showed Santa in jail, looking out through the bars. A boy on the street stares in dismay. It's true! St. Nicholas spent nine years in jail. He was metropolitan bishop of Myra. He was the special friend of children, kind and generous. He fell into disfavor with the emperor, and Diocletian arrested him. He tortured him and then imprisoned him, where he remained until Constantine released him in 312. But Christianity could not be imprisoned. There will always be a Christmas because there will always be a Christ.

Christ was introduced to the world by the name Emmanuel, "God with us." He is not just with us on one day. December 25 may not even have been the birthday of Christ. Others have been observed: November 18, January 6, March 25, and March 28. December 25 was chosen because it was the day pagans worshiped the sun. Christians deliberately chose that as the day to observe Christ's birth saying, "We worship not the sun but the One who made the sun." So Christmas means "God with us" every day of the year.

Christmas also declares that God is for us. We would not want Him with us if we did not know He was for us. Ancient peoples thought that sickness, misfortune, and tragedy were signs that God was angry. They lived in fear. They did not know that God is for us. Christopher Morley once wrote a poem, "To a Telephone Directory." He thought of all the people represented by those phone numbers. He thought of all the bad news they had received over the phone. He wished that he might call every one of them and give them some good news. It is possible to do that. The best of all good news is that God is for us. "Unto you is born this day, a Savior."

It is staggering to think that God is with us. More staggering still is to think He was born of a woman in a stable. Most staggering of all, God is in us.

A man was in Hungary one December helping the refugees from Soviet oppression. He was arrested and jailed. Making a mark each day, he knew when Christmas came. After his release, someone said, "Somebody owes you a Christmas." He disagreed. He said that on Christmas day he had had one wish, had wanted one gift. His diet had been a bowl of thin soup or a bowl of rice. He wanted desperately a piece of meat. When the guard came that day, he had two bowls. One held his thin soup, the other rice. On top of the bowl of rice was a big, fat pork knuckle. It was the first meat he'd seen in three weeks. To himself he said, "Somewhere hidden in this monstrous world in the heart of one cook, one warden, or one guard, the spirit of Christmas still lives."

Someone said that at Christmas, man is almost what God meant him to be. Christmas proclaims the high promise: "God in us."

# CHRISTMAS AWAY FROM HOME
Luke 2:4-6

How many of you were born here? The rest of you will then be celebrating Christmas away from home. Even if you have lived here long enough that it seems like home, most of you will be separated from some members of your family this year. You will not be with your parents, or your children, or your grandchildren.

Some of you will recall a very memorable Christmas away from home. It may be that you were in college or on a vacation trip. It may be that you were in service, and you remember a Christmas when you ate C rations in Korea or Viet Nam. I want to share with you three memorable Christmases away from home. There is a thread that ties the three together.

Hanns Lilje recalls the Christmas he spent in a Nazi prison cell. The commandant took him from his place of solitary confinement to Cell 212, and there he joined two other prisoners. One had a violin, and he played "Silent Night." One had a Bible, and he read the Christmas story. Lilje spoke to them and recalled the sermon he had preached the previous year at Christmas. The text was:

> "The people that walked in darkness have seen a great light. They that dwell in the shadow of death, upon them hath the light shined."

He pointed out that this year when they had none of the decorations, none of the festivities, none of the feasts associated with Christmas, all that they had left was Christmas itself. That, he said, was a promise to which they must cling.

After the Civil War, Phillips Brooks, tired and weary, went to the Holy Land to try to refresh his spirit. On Christmas Eve, he rode by horseback from Jerusalem out to Bethlehem. The sight of that Palestinian village that night made an indelible impression upon him. Later he was to put it into the form of a poem:

> "O little town of Bethlehem, how still we see thee lie!
> Above thy deep and dreamless sleep the silent stars go by;
> Yet in thy dark streets shineth the everlasting Light;
> The hopes and fears of all the years are met in thee to-night."

50

Can we believe that today? A hundred years later, can modern man believe that? Now that we have been to the moon and back—I suppose for those astronauts, orbiting the moon was a most memorable Christmas—can we believe that the hopes and fears of all the years are met in a little Palestinian village in an obscure corner of the world? The answer to that depends upon whether or not we subscribe to the last verse of Phillips Brooks' poem:

"O holy Child of Bethlehem, descend to us, we pray;
Cast out our sin and enter in, be born in us today."

The promise is fulfilled only if Christ is born in us. The announcement of the angels was, "unto you is born this day . . . a Savior, which is Christ the Lord."

Leonard J. Brummett recalls a Christmas he spent in the Philippine Islands. For four or five nights before Christmas, carolers would come to sing at a person's door. They came in groups of three, five, eight, and ten. They sang, and then they expected the homeowner to give them money or candy. If one were a little late in getting to the door, they shouted out impatiently, "Our Christmas, sir. Our Christmas, sir." Brummett said that this "trick or treat" at Christmas bothered him. It seemed to him as if they had turned Christmas upside-down. The next year, he spent Christmas in the United States. When he saw our commercializiation of it, he wondered if maybe we had not turned Christmas upside-down, too. If we forget the promise, then all the presents in the world are meaningless.

All these Christmases away from home set the stage. Our text shows the first Christmas occurred away from home.

"And Joseph also went up from Galilee, out of the city of Nazareth, into Judea, unto the city of David, which is called Bethlehem, (because he was of the house and lineage of David,) to be taxed with Mary his espoused wife, being great with child. And so it was, that, while they were there, the days were accomplished that she should be delivered" (Luke 2:4-6).

It was a Christmas away from home for Mary and Joseph. The distance from Nazareth to Bethlehem does not seem far to us. To them, it may as well have been the other side of the world. They left their home province with which they were familiar, passed through another, and at last came to Judea. The scenes and streets were unfamiliar to them. They were forced to go. In

Bethlehem they knew no one. Had there been friends or relatives there, they surely would have partaken of their hospitality. With very limited funds, they searched for a place to stay. The signs said, "No Vacancy." With what desperation they must have tried to find some accommodation for the night. Have you ever been sick away from home? Perhaps some of you have even had the experience of giving birth to a child far from home. You have some idea of how Mary and Joseph felt. They had little money, no job, no friends, and no home.

For Christ, the first Christmas occurred away from home. He was used to the company of angels. Now He was in the company of cattle. He was used to walking golden streets. Now He would be carried down dusty roads. Even the finest that earth could have offered would have been a poor comparison to Heaven. If Christ had been in a palace or a mansion amid pomp and ceremony with wealth and comfort, even then it would have been a tremendous come-down from Heaven. As it was, He was born amid the poorest earth offered. Yet in His homelessness, we have our home.

"To an open house in the evening
Home shall men come;
To an older place than Eden
And a taller town than Rome;
To the end of the way of the wandering star,
To the things that cannot be, and are;
To the place where God Himself was homeless,
And all men are at home."

—G. K. Chesterton

Why is it that at this time of year so many people go to Bethlehem? Tourists by the thousands will make pilgrimages there this Christmas. Is it not because Bethlehem seems in some sense to be the home of the soul? In His homelessness, we find our home.

For the Wise-men, the first Christmas occurred away from home. They were separated from their families by many miles. They were probably misunderstood and thought fools by family and friends back home. They were in a distant and strange place where they had to ask directions. Never did men come so far to do so little. After weeks of journeying, what did they do? They presented their gifts, they stood in a few moments of worship and adoration. Then there was nothing left to do but

52

go home. Never did men come so far to do so little—and have it mean so much to future generations.

There is a sense in which all of us have always kept Christmas away from home. This world is not our home. I thank God for that. This world with its loneliness, its heartaches, its pain, its sickness, its hate, its trials, and its death is not our home. God did not make us for these clay houses, for this little planet stuck off in a tiny corner of the universe. God made us for himself.

Always at Christmas, we think of home. Each of us has a little different picture. I want to share with you the picture in my heart. It's of a little farm house. There is snow on the ground. Inside there is a tree, but no lights; a few presents, none expensive. There is always enough to eat and rarely enough of anything else. There is a roaring fire to offset the cold wind that finds every crack in that old house. The signs of poverty are there. The unmistakable signs of love are there. Some of you have a memory like that. For others it is far different.

But I have another picture in my heart today. It's of a mansion on a golden street. There's no poverty there. There's no hardship there. There's no uncertainty there. There is boundless and eternal love. Someday, I'm going to celebrate Christmas at home. I'm thinking of a long list of people, members of this church whom we have known and loved, who last year celebrated Christmas with us and who this year will keep Christmas at home. Do you have a hope like that?

# JOY TO THE WORLD
John 15:11

"Why don't your disciples fast?" they asked Jesus. "The disciples of John the Baptist fast. The Pharisees fast. Why don't your disciples fast?" That's the question the old generation always hurls at the new. That's the question that tradition always asks of innovation. That's the question custom always asks of invention. We do not like to have the familiar questioned, challenged, or changed. We want things to go on in the comfortable pattern with which we feel at home.

Jesus' answer, though, is what particularly interests us. He replied, "Can wedding guests mourn?" Christ presents himself as the bridegroom and our union with Him as the wedding, and that is always an occasion for joy.

Our hymnal lists thirty-nine hymns under *Joy*. The word *joy* appears sixty-two times in the New Testament. It appears in connection with the birth of Christ. It appears in connection with the conduct of Christ. It appears in connection with the parables of Christ. It appears in connection with the resurrection of Christ. It appears in connection with the second coming of Christ. It appears in connection with our presentation before the throne of God. In the Gospels and in the epistles, from the beginning of the New Testament to the end, it is joy, joy, joy! Such is the theme of our text:

"These things have I spoke unto you, that my joy might remain in you, and that your joy might be full" (John 15:11).

Notice that the Christian's joy is complete: "That your joy might be full." The sinner's joy is incomplete. It is partial. The Bible never denies that there is pleasure in sin. Indeed, we are told Moses refused "the pleasures of sin." We are told that the sinner is one who lives in pleasure. The Bible does not deny that there is pleasure in sin, but the Bible makes it clear that it is partial and incomplete. There is a discord in its songs, a blight on its flowers, a cloud over its sunniest hour.

The complete joy of the Christian is described by a word that means "cheerful, calmly happy." *Cheerful* describes an attitude toward life, a way of looking at things. *Calmly happy* does not suggest giddiness, frivolity, or even gaiety. *Calmly happy* describes a deep and lasting sort of joy—that is the Christian's joy.

It is complete because of its wide scope. The Christian's joy is the joy of accomplishment. In Luke 10:17, the disciples returned from having been sent by Jesus two-by-two into the places where He himself would come. They were sent with power over diseases and devils. They returned with joy and reported, "Lord, even the devils are subject unto us through thy name."

There is nothing like the joy of Christian accomplishment. There is a joy in knowing that you have helped convert a sinner. There is a joy in knowing that you helped comfort a saint. There is a joy in sharing Christian truths you've learned with someone else. There is a joy in seeing your Sunday-school class grow, in seeing your church grow. God gives us the joy of spiritual accomplishment. It runs deeper than the joy of personal accomplishment, for it is an unselfish joy. It is healthier because it is not based in vanity or conceit. It is a humble joy.

There is the joy of discovery. Jesus said, "The kingdom of heaven is like unto treasure hid in a field; the which when a man hath found, he hideth, and for joy thereof goeth and selleth all that he hath, and buyeth that field." New converts are often exuberant in a way that baffles older Christians. It is the joy of discovery. And the new convert is also baffled—by the blasé attitude of the older Christian. He has discovered something. Imagine how the diver feels when in the murky depths he finds the sunken ship, the hidden treasure. Imagine how the archaeologist feels when his spade hits the long-lost object he has sought. Imagine how the scientist feels when his microscope suddenly reveals the long-sought virus. These are the joys of discovery. To the Christian, there is the highest joy because he has made the highest discovery. He has discovered in personal experience that God is real. He has discovered in personal experience that God forgives. He has discovered in personal experience that God answers prayer.

There is a joy of companionship. Remember that Jesus said it was "like a wedding." Think of that. Men and women rejoice in a wedding because it is an end of loneliness, a beginning of companionship.

Just after her twentieth wedding anniversary, Mrs. Dwight Morrow sat at dinner next to Paderewski, the great pianist. He had played at her alma mater, and Paderewski asked her if she often returned there.

She said, "Yes, I like to go back and sit in my old chapel seat, thinking how much happier I am now than I ever thought I should be."

Paderewski was amazed that she could be happier now than she thought she'd be at eighteen. "Mrs. Morrow," he said, "I want to meet your husband."

The companionship of Christ is like that. It is like marriage at its best, marriage at its ideal.

People change; Christ never changes. Death separates us from people, never from Him.

Christian joy is a lasting joy. "That my joy might remain in you," Jesus said. Just before the cross, Jesus said, "And ye now therefore have sorrow: but I will see you again, and your heart shall rejoice, and your joy no man taketh from you" (John 16:22). It worked out just that way. Jesus rose from the dead and appeared to His followers. Faith filled their hearts with joy. They went gladly across the world with the good news of the resurrection. To them it was not drudgery, but high privilege. To them it was not duty, but a glorious opportunity. God gave them a lasting joy that even death could not take away.

Gypsy Smith, the great evangelist, riding with a friend on a train, said, "Isn't it wonderful to be a soul winner for Jesus." No sooner had the words been spoken that the train wrecked and Gypsy Smith was killed. The last words he spoke were a biography of his life. "Isn't it great to be a soul winner." His joy lasted as long as life.

Why is this such a lasting joy? Because it is a fruit of the Spirit. Paul said in Galatians 5:22, "The fruit of the Spirit is love, JOY, peace." This joy does not come from some joke or anecdote, some humorous situation, some entertainment, or some diversion. It comes from the Holy Spirit of God. When He dwells within us, we have joy.

That explains why some Christians do not seem to have this joy. They are quenching the Spirit. They are not letting the Spirit reign in their lives. God wants them to have joy. God wants you to be happy. And God knows you will be happiest when you are in His will, following the leading of His Spirit.

Moses recognized that he could only enjoy the pleasures of sin "for a season." No one knows how long or how short that season will be. It may be a week, a month, a year, or a decade. Still there comes the time when sin no longer pleases. Eventually, there must come a time when the sweetest cup turns bitter; sooner or later, one gets to the dregs in the bottom of the cup. Sin leads from disappointment to disaster to despair.

Sin is sad. Sin never appears to be sad in the beginning. That's because the devil is a liar. He is a deceiver, and so sin in the beginning never appears to be sad. Indeed, it appears to be quite the opposite. However, sin is sad, basically—at its heart. Sin is sad, ultimately in its results. Sin is sad basically because it involves a cleavage between man and his Maker. It builds a wall between man and God. The result is an indescribable loneliness, a deep, spiritual loneliness. Man was made to walk and talk with God. When a man discovers that he can no longer pray—when he discovers that he no longer walks arm in arm with the One who made him—he experiences an incredible loneliness. He may not at the first know what is wrong, but he knows beyond question that something is wrong. Thus, sin is sad basically, at its very heart.

Sin is sad ultimately in that it bears bitter fruit. The fruit of sin is enslavement. The first time you commit a sin, you do it because you may. The last time you do it because you must. Sin is sad because it is so disappointing. No sin ever looks as good in retrospect as it did in prospect. The sin we committed yesterday never looks as good as the sin we are tempted to commit today. This disappointment that comes over and over and over again finally breeds a kind of cynicism about life itself. One concludes that all of life is disappointing.

We begin to reflect upon others our feelings about ourselves. If we are unreliable, we conclude that everybody else is unreliable. If we lie, we trust no one. If we steal, we trust no one. If we are disloyal, we look upon all men as traitors. This is the bitter fruit of sin, and it makes it inexpressibly sad.

But the Christian knows complete and lasting joy. This joy is an unconditional joy. I do not mean that there are not internal conditions to be met. I mean it is not subject to the external conditions of life. To be sure, it is conditional in the sense that faith and living in the will of God and letting His Spirit rule are essential to such joy. I speak now of the external conditions of life: poverty or wealth, sickness or health, good times or bad, failure or success. Our joy is not conditioned by any of these.

How do I know that? Because Jesus described it as "my joy." His was a joy in the face of poverty, a joy in the face of suffering, a joy in the face of discouragement, of disappointment, of failure.

Jesus speaks of "my joy." A lot of people never think of Jesus as being happy. The only verse they ever memorized was, "Jesus wept." They think that was characteristic of His life. If it had been, do you suppose He would have been a welcome guest at the banquet tables of publicans and sinners? If Jesus did not lead a happy life, then this text means nothing. ". . . my joy in you."

Do you suppose that Jesus sat around at those feasts with a long, sad face, as if all of life were one long wake? Don't you think He threw back His head and roared with laughter? Don't you think He greeted people with a warm smile? If Jesus' life is an example of this perfect life, it must have been filled with joy. I do not mean to suggest that Jesus was frivolous. I do not mean to suggest that Jesus did not regard life as serious business. But he who understands life cannot help but sometimes see the humor in it. The person who is never amused has no real grasp of the meaning of things. You cannot view life as it really is, or man as he really is, without sometimes breaking out into laughter. People welcomed Jesus wherever He went because He had a cheerful attitude toward life.

We wonder how James could say, "Count it all joy when you fall into trials of every sort." How, we wonder, could we rejoice in trials? He does not mean that we rejoice because of our trials. That would be foolish and unrealistic. No man rejoices because he is sick, rejoices because he is in pain, or rejoices because he must die. But even in the face of these unwelcome events, I can rejoice. I can rejoice in the knowledge that trials are temporary. I can rejoice in the knowledge that Christ endured more. I can rejoice in the knowledge that Christ is with me. I can rejoice in the strength He gives to bear what must be borne.

Paul said to the Corinthians, "I am exceeding joyful in all our tribulation" (2 Corinthians 7:4).

Said the blind hymn writer, Fanny Crosby, "Don't waste any sympathy on me. I am the happiest person living."

I can rejoice because of tomorrow. Jesus promised that "your sorrow shall be turned to joy."

Paul said that he intended to "finish his course with joy."

That takes great faith. But since we must all come to the finish line someday, let us learn to cross it courageously, yes, even joyfully. Jesus did.

Perhaps the most remarkable text in the New Testament is Hebrews 12:2: "Jesus ... who for the joy that was set before him endured the cross." Jesus could face death with joy! Not that Jesus welcomed death—Gethsemane shows He clung to life as we cling to life. Not that Jesus was morbid or unreal, but that Jesus looked beyond death into life—and the joys of life eternal sustained Him in that dark hour of death.

John Hus, asked by pope and emperor to deny his faith, refused. From his prison cell he wrote: "I write this in prison and in chains, expecting tomorrow to receive sentence of death, full of hope in God.... I will, this day, joyfully die." That is the supreme accomplishment of the human soul. "I will, this day, joyfully die."

There is also the larger joy beyond life here. To the faithful servant in Jesus' parable the householder said, "Enter into the joys of thy Lord." Someday we will leave the joys of this life for the larger joy of Heaven.

In the quiet of the evening
 As I lay me down to rest,
My soul went out in longing
 For the homeland of the blest.

And I almost saw the city
 With the loved ones waiting there,
And the burdens of life grew lighter,
 As I breathed my evening prayer.

John M. Baker entitled that poem "Homesick for Heaven!"

# NO ROOM
John 1:1-14

"And she brought forth her firstborn son, and wrapped him in swaddling clothes, and laid him in a manger; because there was no room for them in the inn" (Luke 2:7).

"There was no room for Christ in the inn, when He was born; there was no room for Him in Nazareth when He began to preach. There was no room for Him in the temple when He declared Himself to be the Son of God. There was no room for Him in the empire when He declared Himself to be a king. At the last, there was no room for Him on earth, and they suspended Him above it on a cross" (Eldersveld).

The text is, of course, only a simple statement of fact, that the village inn was too small for those who thronged it that day. But the text suggests an idea that goes far beyond that. The religious institutions of Jesus' day had no room for Him because they were too narrow. They were concerned only with people of their own blood, with people who shared the same heritage. Is it possible that the religious institutions of our time likewise have no room for Him, because they have become too small, too narrow, too much concerned with self? Have we allowed them to shrink until there is no room in them for a universal Christ—for a Christ who loves all men, men who are not like us? Have we allowed the church to turn inward rather than outward? Is the church concerned only with the perpetration of its own life and machinery?

And what of our hearts? Have they become too small for Him? Is there room in our hearts for the kind of Christ the Bible talks about? Is there room in our hearts for the true spirit of Christmas?

Not far from a certain place of worship there was a rather expensive signboard declaring that the Spirit of Christmas is "Four Roses." Some of you will know that Four Roses doesn't come from a florist. It may come as some surprise to you to learn that the spirit of Christmas comes in a bottle! Ah, those bottles are destructive to everything Christmas is here to create. The spirit of Christmas is "peace on earth." In thousands of homes, the peace of the family will be destroyed this Christmas by alcohol. The peace of mind of thousands will be ruined by alcohol. The peace of the community will be disturbed because of alcohol. The spirit of Christmas is goodwill toward men. How many men of goodwill will be turned to men of ill will this Christmas because of alcohol? How many dollars that might have been usefully spent will be wasted! The spirit of Christmas? It is almost blasphemy to say that! The spirit of Christmas is love, joy, peace, giving, and forgiving. For these it takes a large heart indeed. If you have an enlarged heart physically, you may not regard it as any particular blessing; but spiritually, we all need to have enlargement of the heart.

We may well ask today, "What is it that shrinks the heart so that we forget the joy of giving and the greater joy of forgiving? What is it that shrinks the heart so that there is no longer any room for the peace that passes understanding? What is it that shrinks the heart so that no longer can we even know love or at the last even know joy?" Everyone of us can answer that question. We can answer the question in one word: "Sin." Sin shrinks the heart and shrivels the human soul so that there is no room for the Christ of Bethlehem, the Christ of the Bible!

Yes, there was no room in the inn, or in the temple, or in the empire, or in the heart. We would have been surprised if there had been. What kind of Christ would we have if He could have been confined in a little village inn? If He could have been contained within a little, narrow national religion? If He could have been controlled by some military empire? What kind of Christ would He be? We would be surprised if there had been room enough for Him anywhere, for the Christ we serve is too great ever to be confined! He is too great to be ignored, as He will be by so many. There is a text that I want to call to your attention. It is the words of the Wise-men who came to Jerusalem. They asked, "Where is He that is born King of the Jews?" Think about it. Where is He? Wise men still ask it. Let's ask it of our celebration of Christmas. "Where is He?"

Imagine being invited as a guest to a birthday party, and you ask, "Who is having the birthday?" Everyone says, "None of us." Why are you having a birthday party if the guest of honor is not present? Why does the world have birthday parties in celebration of the birth of Christ when He is not there? Indeed, everyone would be most embarrassed if He were there!

Where is He that is born when we are celebrating His birthday? Where is He in our nation? Is ours truly a Christian nation? Does our nation really care what Christ thinks about our national life? Does our nation really seek the wisdom of Christ in determining our national policy? You know and I know, beyond all question, we try to keep Him out of our national life. It would be embarrassing for Christ to know how we run this country.

Where is He in our homes? Santa Claus will be in nearly every home this Christmas. Christ will be invited into only a few. Everywhere they will sing "Jingle Bells" and read 'Twas the Night Before Christmas, or Charles Dickens' Christmas Carol. In how many homes will they read Luke chapter 2?

Where is He in our homes at Christmas? For that matter, where is He in our homes anytime? Where is He in our churches? You can worship in a different church next Sunday and not hear the name of Christ once. If you pick churches properly, you can go to a different church for fifty-two Sundays, and Christ will not be mentioned for a year. May God save us from seeing that ever happen in this place! May we be determined that Christ will always be in our church, preached from our pulpit, taught in the classes, revered in our hearts.

Yes, Christ is too great to be ignored; yet we live in a world that seems determined to ignore Him.

Those early Wise-men were astrologers; they studied the stars. The stars led them to Christ, but when they found Christ, they worshiped Him. Now humanity is walking that same road, backward. Now humanity forsakes Christ and seeks again to find in the stars their guidance for life. There are far too many who take the stars seriously, but who do not take the Savior seriously. The Wise-men forsook the wisdom of the star in favor of worshiping Christ. Not only is He too great to be ignored, He's too great to be dismissed with a gesture, with a polite little nod, with a mere tip of the hat.

It's our custom in many cities to have a Santa Claus parade. There isn't anything wrong with that. I'm in favor of that, but there's one part about it we ought to change. Often, a representative of the local ministerial association is asked to have an invocation. Now you imagine about four or five hundred children, yelling and screaming, gathered around Santa Claus, and then we say, "We're going to have an invocation"! It is a travesty, and ought to be left out, because Christ is not to be dismissed with a gesture. It is my judgment that it is better to have no prayer at all than to have a prayer like that.

Every once in a while, I go to some function, and they call on me to have a little prayer. That's one thing you can't have. There is no such thing as a little prayer. There is such a thing as a brief prayer. Some of them in the Bible had only two or three words, and it's perfectly all right to have a brief prayer. There are times when a brief prayer is a whole lot more religious than a long prayer. You *can* have a brief prayer, but the one thing you can *never* have is a little prayer. If it reaches God, it has a magnitude beyond description; and if it doesn't reach God, then it isn't a prayer at all.

Oh, let's not dismiss Christ with a nod or with a polite gesture, and nothing more. He's too great for that! Christ is also too great to be expected to compete. He must compete at Thanksgiving with a turkey and at Christmas with Kris Kringle and on Easter with new hats and bunny rabbits. Isn't it strange that we take all of the holy days, rob them of all of their meaning, and then hang our tinsel and our trinkets on a hollow shell.

So great is our Lord that Solomon said of Him, "The heaven and heaven of heavens cannot contain thee" (1 Kings 8:27). We need that kind of view of our Lord and of His Christ. There could never be room for Christ on earth. He's too great for our little world. He's too much for our little planet. There will never be room for Him, not the Christ of the New Testament.

The Bible speaks of us as those "upon whom the ends of the world are come" (1 Corinthians 10:11). Oh, don't you see the greatness of that? John, who began his Gospel with those stirring words from our Scripture lesson this morning, "In the beginning was the Word, and the Word was with God, and the Word was God.... And the Word was made flesh, and dwelt among us," ends his Gospel with this: "And there are also many other things which Jesus did, the which, if they should be written every one, I suppose that even the world itself could not contain the books that should be written." That sounds like a great exaggeration, doesn't it? But think about it. All we know about Christ happened before He was twelve and after He was thirty. So there are eighteen years about which we know nothing. Write everything Jesus said and did through thirty-four years. Then show how everything Jesus did related to the prophecies of the Old Testament. Then show how Jesus' words and deeds affected the life of His own time. Then discuss how Jesus' life has affected all subsequent history, how men's minds have been changed by the gospel of Christ. Put all that down and you've got a lot of books. Then start writing about the meaning of Christ, the nature of Christ, what it means for Him to be the Son of God and Son of man, what it means for Him to be the Lion of the tribe of Judah, and what it means for Him to be the Lamb of God. John is not exaggerating when he says that the world could not contain the books if you wrote down everything that concerned Jesus of Nazareth. If the world could not contain the chronicle of the Christ, then the world could not contain Christ, either.

There is another side to this truth. As a coin has two faces, there are two sides to this truth. This Christ who is so great that He cannot be contained in our world is also so great that He can never be kept out of our world. People have been trying that since He entered our world. Herod tried to keep Christ out. Where's Herod? He's dead. Indeed, before Jesus had ever grown up to young manhood, the message came: "They are dead which sought the young child's life." When at last He had grown to manhood, Pilate tried to get Him out of our world.

There is an interesting story that concerns Pilate's wife, who, you will remember, warned her husband to have nothing to do with this just man. After the awful events of that night, it is said that she sent for a servant to find out what had become of Christ. The servant said, "He has been let loose in the world."

That's what happened at Bethlehem and at Calvary in the resurrection. Christ was turned loose in the world. The Herods and the Pilates keep on in their futile efforts to get Him out of our world. Communism tries to shut Christ out of the world. Though they hold half the world's people in their thrall, in little groups beneath the hammer and the sickle and in little groups beneath the red star, still the disciples of Jesus are faithful to Him. The soil of Russia and China has already been stained by the blood of martyrs. Communism continues its effort, but it is a futile effort; they cannot keep Him out of our world.

Over here in the free world, we try to keep Him out by means of what is called secularism, by trying to build a non-religious world. It is not necessarily anti-religious at the first, although it may turn out to be at the last. Our world tries to build a society that's neutral concerning Christ. That is the one thing you can never be. Although the world tries desperately to keep Him out, the fact is that the world is full of Him. Read history. Study art. Look at literature. Consider drama or poetry. Even the modern writers, who imagine themselves to be completely divorced from religion, keep coming back to write about the old moral issues that Jesus spotlighted centuries ago.

If it is a fact that we cannot keep Him out of our world, it is also a fact that we cannot escape Him. He keeps confronting us on the busy street corners of life and at the lonely crossroads of life. In the most unexpected places and at the most unexpected times, we suddenly find ourselves gazing into the piercing eyes of the Son of God. He keeps poking into all the dark, musty corners of life, into the closets where the skeletons are. He goes over our books and our bank accounts. He reads our correspondence; He reads our hearts.

This is the Christ I want you to see today—the Christ who could never be kept out and from whom you cannot keep away.

Dr. John Rosen is a very famous psychiatrist who has had remarkable success with people who would not respond to the normal methods of psychiatry. These are the people called catatonics. They refuse to talk to anybody. Many of them go to bed, and they bend their body in the shape that the baby was in the womb.

They refuse to move from that position, and they refuse to speak a single word. Dr. John Rosen tried a new method. He moved in on the ward and put up a cot there. Every day he would go by and see these patients. Then every once in a while, he would stop at a patient's bed, take off his coat and tie, and climb into bed with them! He'd put his arms around them, and gently embrace them. And some of them returned to the world of the living because of that wordless expression of love.

Christmas means that God moved in on the ward. He came into the sickroom of sin in order that He might restore us to spiritual health.

# MISTER X

There is perhaps no more pathetic line in all Scripture than this text: "He was in the world, and the world was made by him, and the world knew him not. He came unto his own, and his own received him not" (John 1:10, 11).

Let us pray. "O Lord, forgive us for the times we fall into that same group of self-satisfied, self-righteous men who ought to have acknowledged thy Son, but who, in fact, rejected Him. Help us to believe that He came to us. Help us to receive Him. Amen."

I am seeing it more and more these days—and I get a little sick every time. Xmas, Xmas, Xmas. Somebody said it was a birthday; so I guess it must be the birthday of Mister X. Who is this man whom the world does not have time to name?

I know, there are those who defend Xmas on the grounds that X is the first letter in the Greek word for Christ and that it stands for Christ. And some have said that because of this, it was an early symbol of Christianity and marked secret meeting places of Christians.

That argument has never sounded convincing to me.

But I personally defend the use of Xmas. I think it is altogether appropriate and right that we should spell it this way. Let me show you why.

In Algebra, X stands for the unknown, and He is today the unknown Christ. Count the billboards advertising liquor. Then hunt for one advertising a church. I leafed through a popular magazine and almost every page was a full-size ad for liquor. Evidently some don't know the difference between Christmas spirit and spirits. Christmas does not come in bottles—not in liquor bottles, nor perfume bottles, nor bottles of shaving lotion.

If He stepped on earth today, would we know Him? Would we know Him? Or would John 1:11 have to be written all over again?

To the student, Christmas means a holiday; to the merchant, a sale; to the child, a present. Is there anybody to whom Christmas means Christ?

Unknown, even at this season in society, He is also unknown in the home. Did you hear about the little boy in Sunday school who was asked where Jesus was born?

He answered, "Philadelphia!"

"No," said the teacher.

"Pittsburgh!"

"No," said the teacher. "It was Bethlehem."

"I knew it was somewhere in Pennsylvania," he said.

In 1247, there was established in London a priory called St. Mary of Bethlehem. A century later, it became a hospital; and by 1401, a hospital for the insane. It is well known that in those days, there was not modern care for the mentally ill. Such places were scenes of noise and confusion. St. Mary of Bethlehem was shortened to Bethlehem and eventually to Bedlam. That's how the word entered our language, and it is there still: bedlam. How is it at your house these days? Is it Bethlehem or bedlam?

Sadly, He is unknown in the church. We have tried too hard to be entertaining—and not hard enough to be enlightening. A little boy had made his first trip to the big top, and he was excited! "Mother," he said, "if you ever go to the circus, you'll never go to church again."

X is an abbreviation, and today He is the abbreviated Christ. Never have I seen it shortened "Christ's." An old Roman said, "The Galilean has been too large for our small hearts." Faced with the choice of enlarging our hearts to receive Him or scaling Him down to our size, we choose the latter.

To some He is still a baby; to others, a teacher, a romantic figure, a name to conjure with, or a name to profane. What is He to you?

X stands for all the sins of omission. They are not, as someone said, "the sins you didn't commit."

X stands for all our attempts to imprison Christ in our own ideas. The Pharisees tried to keep Him within man-made rules. The Zealots tried to confine Him to their political purposes. We, with a Sunday-go-to-meeting Christ, imprison Him behind the stained glass windows.

X is a cancellation mark, and today He is the cancelled Christ. Herod cancelled Him for political reasons. The Sadducees cancelled Him for business reasons. The Pharisees cancelled Him for religious reasons.

There is a little Herod in all of us. We like to be political, in society if not in government. There is also a little of the Sadducee in us. Business or profession comes first. There is a little of the Pharisee in us, too. We like a self-serving religion, one that indicts what we never do and commands what we have already done and ignores what we fail to do.

Christ is regarded as out of date, out of step, and out of place: multiplying His loaves and fishes when no one eats bread at all and fish only on Friday; riding His donkey in the jet age; speaking of love in a world where only money and power talk; urging us to give in a world that takes; talking peace when we all believe that only war can save us!

Once, when Christmas Day fell on a Sunday, church leaders in one congregation actually suggested that church services ought to be cancelled.

In His own day, they cancelled Him, in fact!

Some say the cross may actually have been in the shape of an X. Every time you see Xmas, in your mind adjust that X a little and turn it into the shape of a cross. Adjust your thinking a little to see the real gift of God.

We are not saved by a baby in a manger! We are saved by a man on a cross!

Authors' note: We are indebted to Olin W. Hay for the basic idea and outline of this sermon.

# WHERE IS HE THAT IS BORN?

They were strangers in town. That was obvious from their dress and manner. If Jerusalem was at all surprised to see them, they themselves were quite surprised at what they found. For in Jerusalem, there were no parades, no celebrations, no banners, and no feasts. It was business as usual. They began to ask, "Where is he that is born?"

"Why, there are babies born everyday in Jerusalem. Which one do you mean?"

"Where is he that is born King of the Jews?"

"What? A baby born in Herod's household? Not likely. And a luckless fellow if he is. Already Herod has killed two of his sons to protect his power. I've heard nothing lately of a baby in Herod's house, but maybe you should go to him personally."

In the august presence of the Roman puppet governor, they repeat their question. "Where is he that is born King of the Jews? for we have seen his star in the east, and are come to worship him."

Herod is stunned. A rival for the throne? His advisors suggest that it is perhaps the Messiah. "Where is the Messiah to be born?" asks Herod. He summons the chief priest—calls a cabinet meeting. Rumors soon race through the little capital. "The Messiah has been born," some said. "There is one who claims to be king," said others.

Meanwhile, back at the palace, Herod has learned a little Scripture. For the first time, he reads the prophet Micah, "And thou Bethlehem, in the land of Judah, art not the least among the princes of Judah: for out of thee shall come a Governor. . . ." What? ". . . Out of thee shall come a Governor that shall rule my people Israel."

Summoning again the visitors, Herod told them Bethlehem was the place and inquired as to the precise time the star appeared. The Wise-men went to Bethlehem, and Herod went to work to secure his position. After days of worry and nights without sleep, he decided to kill every baby in Bethlehem.

"But what if it is the real Messiah?" his advisors asked. "You would be fighting against God!" Herod silenced them with a look, ordered his troops on their way, and went muttering to his chambers, "No one is going to take away my throne . . . not even God."

"Where is He that is born?" The Wise-men asked it reverently. Herod asked it murderously. Many today ask it cynically. For myself, I ask it of you inquiringly.

Where is He that is born? Such a question points us to the missing Christ.

Jesus was not in Jerusalem when the Wise-men came. You expect to find a king in the capital. That's logical. How strange it seemed to them that He was not there.

He is still a missing person at Christmas. A school teacher was supervising the construction of a nativity scene. The little family was placed in the stable and Jesus in the manger, with the Wise-men on one side and the shepherds on the other. One little boy asked, "What I'd like to know is, where does God fit in?" Ahh! I look at a secular Christmas and cry, "What I'd like to know is, where does God fit in?"

The drunken revelry, the office party where people cannot remember what they did the night before, the illicit adventures, the wild greed, the mad scramble to buy the bargains, the hurt feelings because a card was not sent—I look at it all and ask, "Where does God fit in?"

A little boy had been to Sunday school and was overheard to say on his way home, "Wait till I get home and tell my folks Jesus was born on Christmas. Boy, will they be surprised!"

He is missing in our celebration, missing in our songs, missing on our gift list, missing in our homes, and sometimes even missing in our churches!

That's hard to imagine. You would as readily expect to find Christ in a church as the Wise-men expected to find Him at Jerusalem. And sometimes He is not there. The root is this: He is missing in our hearts.

We must make room for Him. As we never find time for anything, but only make time, so we can never find room for Him. We must make room.

A merchant remarked once to his minister, "What a job! I've got to rid this store of Christmas in one day!"

"My job is harder," said the minister. "I've got to keep Christmas in the people's hearts for a lifetime."

Jesus was not in Jerusalem, where the Wise-men expected to

find Him. He was in Bethlehem, where they did not expect to find Him. Who, after all, would expect to find a king in a village—a tiny obscure little farming village? And who would expect to find a king so poor he had no proper bed, or roof, or home? Rootless and homeless, vagrants stood by His cradle.

For that matter, who would expect the Messiah in the form of a baby? The Messiah might be expected to come as a shining warrior, to come as a crowned king, to come as an angel of light, or to come on wings of cloud and sunlight. But to come as a little crying, burping baby? He is truly the unexpected Christ—always.

You would not have expected to find Him in the temple at twelve, discussing the fine points of the Bible with experts. You would not have expected to find Him at little Nazareth doing a carpenter's work until He was thirty. When He began His ministry, you would not have expected Him to have set up His headquarters in Capernaum. In Rome perhaps, or Athens, or Alexandria in Egypt, and if in Palestine at all, surely in Jerusalem, but in Capernaum? Not even in its more prestigious neighbor-town Tiberias, but Capernaum. That little border village, that customs post, that outpost of empire and nation.

You would not expect to find Him dining in the home of a leper, nor going to be the guest of a publican, nor stopping to talk with a strange and sinful woman by a public well. Always—always—He is the Christ of the unexpected.

Still one finds Him in unexpected places—not among the mighty, but the lowly. If He is sometimes absent from great cathedrals, you will find Him always on skid row, and on the wrong side of the tracks, and among the slums and open sewers of the world. You will find Him among India's poor and Africa's starving.

> In haunts of wretchedness and need,
> On shadowed thresholds dark with fears,
> From paths where hide the lures of greed,
> We catch the vision of Thy tears.
> Where cross the crowded ways of life,
> Where sound the cries of race and clan,
> Above the noise of selfish strife
> We hear Thy voice, O Son of Man.
> —Frank Mason North

Still, still He is the Christ of the unexpected. If you want a humdrum business-as-usual life, don't be a Christian. Faith offers more excitement, more adventure, more that is new and grand than anything else.

The Mellon Hospital in Haiti was not just built by a wealthy scion of the Mellon family. That man went to medical school at an age when many would think it too late. Now he is personally in Haiti, healing with his hands as well as with his fortune and proving again that Jesus is the Christ of the unexpected.

His grace, His forgiveness, His patience with us, His love—all these are unexpected—and undeserved.

He always will be the Christ of the unexpected. He is coming again. Some people have His itinerary all worked out for Him, and they know His timetable. But the Bible says that once again, He will be the Christ of the unexpected.

He is also the inescapable Christ. Where is He? Everywhere. Ever present.

How can I say that He is missing and say that He is ever present? The answer is plain. When I speak of the missing Christ, I am really talking about the unrecognized Christ, the unacknowledged Christ, the unworshiped Christ.

He is at all those Christmas parties where liquor flows like water and people do things of which they would ordinarily be ashamed. He sees. He is present in the board rooms and offices when greed dominates every thought. He sees. He is present in those homes where the only thought is to please the kiddies and somehow pay the bills. He sees. He is present in those hearts where envy and jealous strife and anger rise over some imagined slight. He sees. He is present in those churches that have passed Him by in disbelief—or else have crowded Him out by their Madison Avenue machinery. He sees.

"All things are naked and open before Him with whom we have to do." And "the whole earth is full of His glory." "The heaven and heaven of heavens cannot contain thee." "The world itself could not contain the books."

You can't keep Him out of Christmas. You can't keep Him out of society. You can't keep Him out of business. You can't keep Him out of government. You can't keep Him out of world politics. And you can't keep Him out of your life.

# DO YOU HEAR WHAT I HEAR?
Isaiah 6:9, 10; Matthew 13:14; Acts 28:26

Why is it that you don't always hear what I hear and I don't always hear what you hear?

Sometimes we have lost our keenness of hearing. It is a common enough condition of health that hearing is sometimes impaired. Sometimes it is because of circulation. Sometimes it is nerve damage. Sometimes the ear drum itself is injured. Do people find their spiritual hearing sometimes impaired? Certainly! If it were not so, then every church would have standing room only every Sunday! Some no longer hear, "Come unto me, all ye that labor and are heavy laden."

What is it that impairs our spiritual hearing? It is sin! The Bible speaks of spiritual blindness. To the church at Laodicea Jesus said, "Thou ... knowest not that thou are wretched, and miserable, and poor, and blind, and naked." Commenting on that, someone gave us the well-known quotation, "Sin cuts the optic nerve of the soul." We may describe the same condition in different terms by saying that sin impairs our hearing.

We cannot hear God calling to us. We cannot hear angels announcing the good news. We cannot hear the cry of our brother's need. Yes, sin will impair our spiritual hearing.

That's the use Isaiah makes of this text. And Jesus. And Paul.

Another reason that people do not always hear what others hear is indifference. That which we have heard often we now no longer hear at all.

On their tenth wedding anniversary, a man bought his wife a grandmother clock. It chimed every fifteen minutes, and the first night they had it, they didn't sleep a wink. But after a while, they began to sleep the whole night through and never hear the clock chime. In fact, unless they listened for it, they never heard it at all. But the morning after they had overnight guests, the guests would come out red-eyed and bleary, and the man remembered that the clock struck every quarter hour.

The same thing is illustrated in the person who buys a hearing aid. When he had normal hearing, he simply tuned out the noises he didn't want to hear. He tuned out the wind, the hum of machinery, the cries of birds. Then he became hard of hearing and never heard them at all. Finally he gets a hearing aid, and all those extra sounds come in again! He turns his hearing aid down—so low it does him very little good, to shut out the noises we all hear every day, and yet do not hear. We tune them out. (Some men have even been known to tune out their own wives! Imagine that!)

Does it grow old to you, this gospel story? This so familiar business of shepherds and Wise-men and a baby in a manger? These songs we sing? These sermons I preach? Have you heard it all so often that now you really do not hear it at all? That would be a shame. The clock makes a lovely sound, though its owner never enjoys it! The birds' songs are sweet, even though we never hear them!

There is something about this Christmas business that never grows old. If anything grows dull, it is us! We grow indifferent to the whole thing! Try to imagine today that you are hearing it all for the first time! Hear it with the wonder of childhood! Hear it with the amazement of heathen savages. Hear it as a man from another planet would hear it. Never, never let it lose its wonder!

A third reason we do not all hear the same thing is that we are not trained to listen. I may go to the symphony with a trained musician. Afterward I say, "Wasn't that great?" He says, "Yes, but the second violin was flat." He was trained to hear things that I could not. I take my mechanic for a ride in my car. "Hear that?" I ask. "I hear a lot of things," he said. "I hear some things you don't even hear!" And the acuteness of his trained ear costs me plenty!

It is a fact that to appreciate fully what we are hearing at Christmas, we have to have some training, some preparation. Doubtless, Christmas meant a great deal to the shepherds, but certainly it meant much more to Simeon, that devout man in the temple who had saturated himself with the Word of God.

If we know something about the circumstances of a song, it means more to us. I have enjoyed "Hark, the Herald Angels Sing" far more since I learned how Charles Wesley wrote it, and that it was almost lost forever. I appreciate all the more "While Shepherds Watched Their Flocks by Night" when I know that it was one of the earliest Christian hymns. For a long time it was considered sacrilegious to sing hymns of human composition. Only psalms from the Bible were sung in church. It took a brave Nahum Tate to include this song with fifteen others in a supplement to the hymnal with only words of Scripture for songs. At first rejected, the hymn has become a favorite to many. Knowing the background enhances my appreciation for the song.

So he who knows the Old Testament appreciates all the more the New. So he who has read the prophets is better prepared to receive the Prince of Peace.

Any book is more appreciated when the reader knows the author. That may explain why some people get so much from reading the Bible. That may explain why others get so little!

There is a fourth reason why one does not hear what others hear. Sometimes we tend to hear what we want to hear. A lady used to come out of church each Sunday and say, "You did it again!" The preacher didn't know whether to say, "Thank you," or, "I'm sorry." If it was a day he felt good, he took it as a compliment. If it was a day he felt inferior and incompetent, he took it as a complaint. We do tend to hear what we expect.

One minister's column a while back reported that he had heard a lot of impatient customers snarling at short-tempered clerks at Christmas. And the clerks snarled back at the customers. I really hadn't noticed that, until he called my attention to it. I had just been thinking how extra polite and friendly people seemed to be at Christmas. Strangers say, "Merry Christmas!" Merchants smile, and well they should at today's prices! Sometimes drivers even let me in when I am waiting to get into the stream of traffic. It had seemed to me that people were extra nice at Christmas. Now I am noticing instead all the discourteous things people do!

The fifth factor in hearing is competition. Sometimes noise drowns out what we want to hear. You could not tune a piano in an automobile factory. The First Christian Church at Largo, Florida, erected its building with its back to the street, so to speak. Some thought that didn't look too friendly. They said it looked much more inviting for the great open doors to face the highway. They were right, of course. But the church was thinking about the noise. They thought it would be distracting every time someone opened the doors to come in—all that noise of autos rushing by, carrying thoughtless people to insignificant destinations as they roared past the place of worship!

Does Christmas get drowned out in all the noise of "Season's Greetings" and "Holiday Cheer"? By the way, save all those cards you get that say "Season's Greetings." You can send them any time! They say absolutely nothing. When hunting season opens, send one to someone: "Season's Greetings." When baseball season opens, send one to a sports fan: "Season's Greetings." Such cards, intended to say nothing offensive, end up saying nothing at all.

I know of a man who worked at an electric generating plant. It was a very noisy place. He got in the habit of speaking a certain way in the plant, and it carried over into the rest of his life. You might imagine that he got into the habit of shouting, but you would be wrong. He got into the habit of whispering. He knew it was useless to try to shout over the noise of the generators. When he wanted to talk to a co-worker, he would get very near to the man and whisper.

That became such a habit that he spoke softly even at church. He would come out after the service, lean over close to the preacher's ear, and whisper very confidentially, "That was a good sermon." At first the preacher thought he didn't want anybody else to know he thought it was good!

God recognized that you can't outshout the world. So in the Old Testament, God speaks not in wind, earthquake, or fire, but in a still, small voice.

And it is so with Christmas. No trumpets in Bethlehem. No heralds for the king except the herald angels, and they appear only to shepherds. No pomp. No parade. Phillips Brooks describes it: "How silently, how silently."

Now with that lengthy background, let us again ask, "Do you hear what I hear?" If our ears are sharp from good spiritual health, if our hearing is not made less acute by indifference, if the best sounds are not drowned out by noise, if we are trained to listen, and if we really want to hear, what can we hear this Christmas—or any Christmas?

I hear a sigh, a sob, and a song!

The sigh comes up from the world itself. It is as if all the earth were in the position of Israel in Egypt long ago. God said, "I have surely seen the affliction of my people which are in Egypt, and have heard their cry." And again He said, "The cry of the children of Israel is come unto me."

So I doubt not that God hears the sighing of a weary world. Can you hear it, too? It is a world tired of tyrants and weary of war! It is a world fatigued by the threats that surround it. It is a world surfeited with the blood that has stained its soil again and again.

Can you hear the sigh, too? Don't tune it out! Painful as it is to hear it, we must not tune it out. The one thing the church dare not do is turn off its hearing aid and refuse to listen to the sighing of a weary, weary world.

To the sighing, God has something to say, something to say to the world through the church. Listen to the sigh.

For some, the sigh becomes a sob. Some will live out this Christmas the awful story of Matthew chapter 2. It will not be a mad king Herod who brings them sorrow. It will be a drunken driver on the highway! It will be a thieving intruder in the night. It will be some thoughtless, careless person. But the pain will be the same.

So often, our only response is, "Don't cry!" There's precious little comfort in that! This Christmas, as at every Christmas, there will be those who have every reason to cry. For some, it will not be quite so sad as death—but almost. For some, this Christmas will mark the death of a marriage; for some, the death of a friendship; for some, the loss of a job with no prospect for a new one; for some, a feared diagnosis made positive.

Yes, for some, the sounds of Christmas will be a sob, and the holiday will be wrapped in black.

We have to hear that! To ignore it would be heartless! To pass it off without notice would be cruel.

But above the sigh and above the sob is a song! And when I ask, "Do you hear what I hear?" I am thinking most of all of the song. The song reassures the sighing and comforts the sobbing. It comes just when we needed a song the most. It comes just when we thought we could never sing again! It comes with its age-old message of comfort and hope. The song comes when it is needed most, as it first came when it was needed most. When it seemed God had forgotten both His people and His promises, the Savior came—and with Him, a song!

"It came to pass in the days of Caesar Augustus, . . ." in days when an emperor in Rome could push people about in the far-flung provinces like pawns on a chess board. He came "in the days of Herod the King," in days when success after success seemed to crown the head of a sinning, cruel, heartless, murdering king.

Jesus came into the world just when the world needed Him most! "In the fulness of time," says the Bible, He came.

He began His ministry just when it was needed most. The Bible says that after John was arrested, Jesus came preaching. The timing was not accidental. Evil had done its worst. God's one fearless spokesman was silenced, and it looked as if right was forever on the scaffold, and wrong was forever on the throne. Then, then Jesus came preaching.

During His ministry, He kept saying, "My time is not yet come; my time is not yet come." Then one night in the Garden of Gethsemane, Jesus said to His disciples, "Behold the hour is coming," and He went to the cross.

So Christmas comes round to us each year just when we were about ready to give up. We were about ready to give up on man, and we were about ready to give up on God. Then there comes again that immeasurably reassuring song.

> Still thro' the cloven skies they come,
> With peaceful wings unfurled,
> And still their heavenly music floats
> O'er all the weary world:
> Above it's sad and lowly plains
> They bend on hov'ring wing:
> And ever o'er its Babel sounds
> The blessed angels sing.
>
> And ye, beneath life's crushing load,
> Whose forms are bending low,
> Who toil along the climbing way
> With painful steps and slow,
> Look now! for glad and golden hours
> Come swiftly on the wing;
> O rest beside the weary road,
> And hear the angels sing!
> —Edmund H. Sears

# A MAN FOR ALL SEASONS
Matthew 1:1-17

"The book of the generations of Jesus Christ, the son of David, the son of Abraham. Abraham begat Isaac; and Isaac begat Jacob; and Jacob begat Judah and his brethren; and Judah begat Pharez ... and Eliud begat Eleazar; and Eleazar begat Matthan; and Matthan begat Jacob; and Jacob begat Joseph the husband of Mary, of whom was born Jesus, who is called Christ."

I've greatly abbreviated it, of course. If I read the whole thing to you, you would be bored to tears. Unless, of course, your name happened to be in the list. And then you would know that it is more than a list of names. These are real people, who lived and loved and laughed and wept, just as we do. In this long list of very real people, we can find the credentials of Christ. We turn often to those other credentials where the Father said from Heaven, "This is my beloved Son in whom I am well pleased." Or John 3:16, the "only begotten Son" of God. Or we have turned often to the story of the virgin birth. I used to preach every Christmas Sunday a sermon on the virgin birth, and that's important. But it's also important to know where Jesus came from on His mother's side. It's important for us to know that He who was both the offspring of David and the Bright and Morning Star is also the Son of man and the Son of God. So we have here, in the first chapter of Matthew, Jesus' family tree.

Suppose I brought with me today my own family tree. It probably wouldn't interest you too much. But suppose there was someone famous in my ancestry--a war hero or a president or something. You might listen to me brag about that. When you grow up in poverty and obscurity, you tend to cling to a little shred of dignity—a little shred of fame like that. That's the way Joseph and Mary were. They had the same lineage up to a point. They were distantly related—not close enough to be a problem—but they were related. They were both descended from David the king. Living as they did, in poverty and obscurity, Joseph and Mary clung to this little shred of dignity and

79

fame. They were descended from the king, and there was royal blood in their veins.

Another thing about a family tree is that there may be a name of one infamous as well as famous on it. Suppose there was a notorious outlaw or a traitor in my ancestry. We wouldn't talk about him too much. Perhaps there is a bad apple on your family tree, too. There were four on Christ's. When you read this genealogy, you discover a surprising thing. There are four women's names. Ordinarily women were not listed in the genealogies of the Old Testament, but there are four of them named here, and there is something shady about every one of them.

One of them is Bathsheba. We all know about her. While her husband was away in service, she was carrying on with the king. There's Rahab. The Bible just plainly labels Rahab a harlot, which has always been the most despised of all occupations. There's Tamar. Tamar was not only guilty of adultery, but incest, in that she had a child by her own father-in-law. She's on the list. The only one that comes through well is Ruth. Ruth's character is fine, but Ruth put herself in a compromising position that could have been a great embarrassment to her and to Boaz, who later became her husband. So she doesn't get off scot-free either. These are the four women who were named in the genealogy of Jesus. It's surprising, isn't it. The world's one perfect man came out of a family like that. More surprising still, they're listed. You would think, conditions being as they were, they just wouldn't say anything about it. But the writer goes out of his way to drag these names in. Why do you suppose that he does that? I don't know for certain, of course. But the fact that they are there is to me a great comfort. If you have ever been ashamed of your family, or if you have ever been ashamed of yourself, it's a great comfort to read this chapter.

It's a great encouragement, too. We can overcome all kinds of handicaps and all kinds of backgrounds. God has overruled appearances before. He can overrule appearances again. We can't sit around making excuses, saying, "Well, I didn't have a fair start in life; so that's the reason that I have done this or that."

Most importantly, there is a great lesson here. Jesus came to identify himself with a human family, a family just like mine, a family just like yours, a family with its good and with its bad. Sometimes we talk about Christ's deity in a way that it seems almost to set Him aside from our world, as if He were on the outside looking in. In fact, He experienced life as we do. All this long experience of history was in Jesus' ancestry. Yet He became the only pure, the only perfect, man who ever lived. It's important for us to know that Jesus had a family, and not just on paper, either. Jesus had a real family. He grew up in a home where there was a mother and where there was a stepfather and where there were half brothers and half sisters. The Bible tells us that His brothers did not believe in Him. We know that Jesus was conscious of His destiny at least from the time He was twelve years old, perhaps sooner. Can you imagine the conflict that must have been in that home in Nazareth—Jesus growing up knowing who He was, and His brothers and sisters not believing who He was. Here was the great Son of the living God, subject to all this conflict and tension. It makes one think of Abraham Lincoln. We put him down as one of the greatest men who ever lived. Yet Abraham Lincoln at home was in a situation of constant tension and conflict because of his unsympathetic wife.

In Jesus' family, it was the brothers and sisters. They dragged Jesus' mother into it, too. You remember once during His ministry that His mother and His brothers came and tried to persuade Him to come back home. I think I know what was in the mother's heart. I think she said, "He's working too hard. He's going to kill himself if He doesn't take it easier. He's working too hard." I think the brothers said, "He's making a fool out of himself, and we've got to persuade Him to come home."

Do you live in a home filled with tension? It would be an unusual congregation if there were not someone in that situation. Jesus understands. Do you live in a home that knows poverty? Jesus understands. Do you live in a home that is afflicted with wealth? Jesus understands that, too. Do you know what it is to live in obscurity? Are you a nobody? Jesus was a nobody until He was thirty years of age and began His ministry. Or have you had to face the opposite problem of fame? Jesus knew the pressure of being famous. Have you succeeded in life? Do you know how difficult it is to live with success? Jesus understands that. Multitudes thronged His feet. Do you know what it is to fail? Jesus experienced failure. Once all but twelve of His followers turned their backs upon Him and forsook Him. Do you know what it is to be betrayed by friends? Jesus did.

There isn't a problem you can name that didn't enter into the life and experience of Jesus. So Christianity has something to say to your situation. I don't know what your situation is, but I know Christ has something to say to it. Christ entered a situation like yours and lived in it.

We've all felt sometimes like the dear old saint who was caught out in a violent thunderstorm. She feared for her life, and she prayed. She said, "Oh Lord, it's no wonder that you have so few friends, if this is the way you treat them." A lot of people have felt like that. But Jesus came into the stormy seas of life and lived through the violent experiences with us. That's a very important thing for us to know.

Then in this list of the ancestry of Jesus, we find the supporting cast for the drama of the ages. There are forty-seven names in the list—the great, the near great, the not-so-great. These forty-seven lives cover two thousand years of history. Here is a history that begins with one man in a nomad's tent on the desert. Then it follows the fortune of a family as they journey back and forth. Then it flows into the experience of a nation, oppressed, delivered, raised to the heights, hurled to the depths. Love, romance, marriage, hate, birth, death, war, murder, peace, wealth, poverty, glory, shame—they are all written here in this panorama of human passion and experience.

At the end of the list is one name, the name above every name, Jesus Christ. This long procession, two thousand years old, stops at Bethlehem. The procession ends at a stable. The procession ends with a baby. Looking back across the long procession, we marvel at the elaborate preparation God made. For Christ was on His way to Bethlehem for centuries. Now we know that God lives and moves in history, making sense out of human nonsense, putting the jig-saw puzzles of life together again and giving purpose to our frustrations and meaning to our failures.

Yes, this is the supporting cast, and Christ is the star. He who is so much a part of our human family was also apart from our human family. For Jesus Christ was absolutely unique. He was not a product of His age or His time. His time produced no other great prophet (except, perhaps, John the Baptist), produced no other great poet, produced no other great preacher who would influence all humanity. Jesus was not the product of His times. He was not the product of His nation. There was little about Israel to suggest that they were to produce a leader such as He. He was not a product of His town, that squalid little town of Nazareth. There was nothing to indicate that from that place would come the Lord of history. Jesus was not the product of His family. The royal blood flowed once in their veins. It was quite diluted when you got down to Joseph and Mary. There was nothing about them to suggest that from such a place should come such a Christ. No, Jesus is not of this world, and His kingdom is not of this world.

We, too, may live apart from this world. That's an inexpressible comfort. That is an immeasurable relief. We can live apart from this world that is so shallow, so superficial—this world that is so unfeeling and indifferent, this world that is so temporal, this world that is so evil. Christ will help us to rise above it and to live apart from it. Truly He was out of this world.

We would imagine that one so unique would have a unique birth, and He did. For though there are thirty-nine begats in this chapter, the most important is the one that isn't there. For when you come down to Christ, Matthew chooses his words very, very carefully. "Matthan begat Jacob; and Jacob begat Joseph the husband of Mary, of whom was born Jesus, who is called Christ." If you want the begat that concerns Jesus, you have to go to John 3:16. "God so loved the world, that he gave his only begotten Son." Above it all, I want you to see that He is the comprehensive Christ—the Man for all the years.

Each year, *Time* magazine selects a man and labels him "The Man of the Year." Sometimes it's a good man, and sometimes it's a bad man. They select the man who, in their judgment, has most influenced the life of the world in that year. He is "The Man of the Year." Pick any year you choose, and Christ is "The Man of the Year." Indeed, He is the "Man of the Years." He is the Man for all seasons. Generations before looked forward to His coming. All generations since look back and wonder. This is the book of the generations of Jesus Christ, the man of all generations. In all the years yet to come, Jesus will still be relevant, and His teachings will still be appropriate. He is the Christ of all ages.

I do not know in what situations you will find yourself in the future, but whatever it is, Christ has something to say to you and for you. I do not know what kind of a shape our world will get itself into in years to come, but I know that Christ will always be there redeeming the world and reclaiming His own. He is the Christ of the ages. He is the Man for all seasons. It would be the greatest of all losses if we should worship Him once a year and turn our attention to Him only at the Christmas season. He deserves something more and something better than that. He is the Man for all situations.

The genealogies run from tents to palaces, from slave-huts to throne rooms, from shepherds to slaves, kings to harlots. So Christ addresses himself to every conceivable human predicament and offers himself as a remedy. Above it all, we see Christ, who has never yielded His control over time, the world, or history. He is the Lord of history.

And we see God busy in history, for twenty centuries, so that you and I could have these few fleeting years of grace. Oh, do not take your privilege lightly. Thank God you were born in such a time as this. God spent two thousand years getting ready for the glory time, in which you and I are now privileged to live. Let us thank God for a Christ who was a product of history, without ever being the victim of it, who belonged to this world, but was not caught up in it. We need such a Savior. We need a Savior who can be the Master of history, who not only lives within it but above it, who directs and controls it while moving along with it. In other words, we need a Savior who is both man and God, one that is truly historical and truly eternal.

We have such a Savior in Jesus Christ! Oh, how our world needs Him—our world so bent on self-destruction. We've threatened ourselves with the atomic bomb; we've threatened ourselves with pollution; we've threatened ourselves with the population explosion. Our world seems bent on physical self-destruction. Our world seems bent on spiritual self-destruction. Into such a world, Christ comes to redeem. "Oh, Holy Child of Bethlehem, Descend to us we pray; Cast out our sin and enter in, Be born in us today."

# AN ARTIFICIAL CHRISTMAS

"Fear not: for behold, I bring you good tidings of great joy, which shall be to all people. For unto you is born this day in the city of David a Saviour, which is Christ the Lord."

Miniature trains on a make-believe track
Carry toy loads to the station and back.
Miniature deer on make-believe snow
Pull toy sleighs as in circles they go.
Miniature trees dot a make-believe hill
While toy stars twinkle all peaceful and still.
Is the happiness false? Is the joy untrue?
Are the peace and love all make-believe too?
In only a moment the carols will start;
Save me, O God, from a miniature heart.

An artificial Christmas, or a genuine Christmas: how can you tell them apart? I'm getting used to artificial Christmas trees. It took some doing, but I've made the adjustment. I no longer have problems with artificial Christmas trees. I have no problem with artificial wreaths; I have no problem with artificial snow. As a matter of fact, I prefer it to the genuine article. And I read somewhere that artificial mistletoe is just as effective as the real thing.

But I have some problem with an artificial Christmas. There are three things that make Christmas artificial and three things that make it genuine.

Christmas is artificial if it is a ritualistic Christmas. It is artificial if we are only doing our spiritual calisthentics, if we are only going through the motions, if we are giving out of duty and if we are going to church out of habit, and if we are singing, not from our hearts, but only from our throats. Anyone who has taken voice lessons should have learned at least one basic principle. That is that one must support the voice on a column of air that comes not from the throat or even the chest, but from deep within. I've learned something else. Spiritually, we must support our songs on something that comes from deep within. How many people who are singing, "Silent night, holy night . . . Christ the Savior is born," neither acknowledge themselves as sinners or Christ as their Savior?

How many people are singing, "O Come All Ye Faithful," and they have no faith at all? So a ritualistic Christmas is an artificial Christmas.

A materialistic Christmas is also an artificial Christmas. Some of my friends preach a lot on Communism and they think I ought to preach on Communism. But I have never met anybody in my ministry that I thought was in danger of becoming a Communist. I have met people that I thought were in danger of becoming materialists. So I prefer to preach on materialism— that's the threat *we* face. Are we, this year, more concerned about Bethlehem Steel than we are about the Bethlehem star? It interests me that every year the news reporters on television interview the merchants and ask, "How is business this Christmas? Is there as much traffic as usual? Are sales up or down?" I've never heard them interview a clergyman and ask whether attendance at church is up or down or whether the people are singing the carols with more gusto this year than before.

Christmas has become so materialistic that some people want to leave Santa Claus out of it altogether. They think it wasn't the Grinch that stole Christmas, but Santa Claus. I read the other day there are three stages in a man's life. First, there is the stage where he believes in Santa Claus. Then there is the stage where he doesn't believe in Santa Claus. Finally there is the stage where he is Santa Claus. I heard about a man whose wife kept nagging him to put in a new concrete patio. He said, "We don't need it, and we can't afford it." She kept insisting and he kept insisting. He talked to his next-door neighbor about it. He said, "I'm just not going to give in." One day, to his astonishment, the neighbor looked out the window, and there was the concrete truck backing up into the back yard. He went over and there stood his neighbor watching them pour that concrete patio. He was all smiles. The neighbor said, "Well, I didn't think you'd do it, and I certainly don't understand what you've got to smile about." The man said, "All her credit cards are in that concrete!"

It's not only in this country that we face a problem of a materialistic Christmas. In England, they have this custom: young people go around the homes and sing carols, not just on one night, but on many nights before Christmas. After they sing carols, they ring the doorbell. When you come to the door, they hold out their hands and say, "Our Christmas, Sir." You're supposed to give them money. Sometimes the first ones arrive as early as the middle of November!

There's a third characteristic of an artificial Christmas. That is, it's a pleasuristic Christmas. Bob Shannon made that word up. You would think with all the words there are in the dictionary, we wouldn't have to make them up, wouldn't you? But I just couldn't find anything that quite fit, so I just used Bob's. But you understand what I mean.

Ritualistic, materialistic, pleasuristic. Surely Christmas is a little bit more than just decking the halls with boughs of holly. Surely it is the season to have some emotion stirring in our breast other than simply to be jolly. The watchword is not "Ho, ho, ho!" It is "Behold, behold, look, see, I bring you good tidings of great joy." You know and I know that there are activities and deeds that are condoned and excused at Christmastime that would never be condoned and excused at any other time of the year. People say, "Oh, well, it's Christmas." They expect people to go into all the kinds of excesses that otherwise are looked down upon, and it becomes pleasuristic.

That's an artificial Christmas. I read about a man who went on a trip to Europe, and nothing satisfied him. The cathedrals were musty and dim; the castles were drafty and damp. He said everything needed paint. Finally they got to Switzerland. They were standing on an overlook, looking out at the magnificent Alps. A beautiful sylvan valley lay in between those snow-capped mountains that reared up against the blue sky. His traveling companion said, "Now, you can't complain about Switzerland, can you?" The man said, "I don't know. Take away the scenery and what have you got?" Of an artificial Christmas one may say, "Take away the scenery and what have you got?"

A genuine Christmas may have the very same scenery; but take away the scenery, and I'll tell you what you've got. First you have something that enriches love. There are people who give to others at Christmas who never give at any other time of the year. There are organizations that are not necessarily benevolent in nature that become benevolent at Christmas. Unabashedly, the Chamber of Commerce is dedicated to commerce. That's what it's for. It's not intended to be a charitable organization. It's dedicated to business, and making it bigger and better. But at Christmas, in many cities, the Chamber of Commerce is gathering food to put in baskets to take to the poor.

Christmas has a way of doing that. Even hearts that have become hard are softened, and hearts that have become cold are warmed. Christmas enriches love. It's a time to give; not simply to give things, but also to give Christmas itself. We have sometimes referred to observing Christmas as "keeping Christmas." Have you ever heard that term used for its observance? Yet, in the ultimate sense, Christmas can never be kept. Always it must be given away. So along with all the other things we are giving this year, let us give Christmas. Christmas itself. It's rather significant, and appropriate, that the first radio broadcast, in 1906, was a Christmas celebration. It was a Canadian, Reginald Aubrey Kessendon, who had been experimenting with voice transmissions by wireless. On Christmas, he broadcast a wireless message to the ships at sea. Sailors in their vessels were startled to hear coming over the instruments not just a code, but a human voice. They heard a violinist play, "O Holy Night." They heard a man read from the Bible from Luke chapter 2. There's a poetic significance in that, for Christmas is always a message to be heard and a message to be told; a message to be given to the world.

A genuine Christmas enriches love. A genuine Christmas nourishes faith. Every time I hear that beautiful song, "Do You Hear What I Hear," another word comes to my mind. A similar sounding word, "fear." Sometime I would like to sing instead of "Do You Hear What I Hear?" "Do You Fear What I Fear?" For fear stalks the world, and faith is the antidote to fear. The shepherds had a message to believe. We too have a message to believe. Faith comes by hearing, and hearing by the Word of God. One of the most magnificent cathedrals in the world is the twin-spired cathedral in Cologne, Germany. It is interesting for more than its architecture. Inside the cathedral there is a magnificent golden box. The gullible believe that in that golden box are the bones of the Wise-men. I don't know whether that's faith or superstition. I don't have much confidence that the bones of the Wise-men are there. But what's important is not the bones of the Wise-men, but the faith that they had. That faith that we can have in all our churches, be they great cathedrals or modest chapels or something in between. A faith that we can have not only in our places of worship, but in our lives. A genuine Christmas nourishes faith.

A genuine Christmas strengthens hope. A minister one year put in his church newsletter this announcement. It was a headline. It said, "An Important Announcement Will Be Made Next Sunday. An announcement that will greatly affect the future of this church." Well, everybody came. They thought he was going to resign. He announced. "Unto you is born this day a Savior." That was one way of getting their attention, but he really shouldn't have got their hopes up like that. Of course, Christmas does get our hope up, in another way, doesn't it?

It came to me a few days ago that one of the most beloved Christmas songs is one that is very little understood because the tune masks the meaning. "God rest ye, merry gentlemen," we sing. I want to go through that a little more slowly today that you may catch something of the impact of it, because it has an enormous impact.

"God rest ye merry, gentlemen,
Let nothing you dismay.
Remember, Christ our Savior
Was born on Christmas Day.
To save us all from Satan's power
When we were gone astray
Oh, tidings of comfort and joy."

Now look at that a little more closely. "God rest ye." That's what we want. "Let nothing you dismay." What dismays you today? What brings you anxiety? Questions of health, questions of economics, family situations, the world at large—what is it that makes you dismayed today? "Let nothing you dismay. Remember Christ our Savior was born on Christmas Day. To save us all." You, me, the folks down the road, the people across the street, the people across the field. "From Satan's power." Only then, when you understand this, do they become tidings of comfort and joy. So your Christmas will be genuine if you think of Satan's power. What an awful thing to suggest at Christmastime. Your Christmas will be genuine if you think of Satan's power and Christ's victory over it. It will be genuine if you think of death and how Christ was victorious over it. That's what makes it genuine.

I have seen some very stunning black and white photographs, but a picture that was only black or only white would be nothing. Only when the black and white come together do you see the beautiful picture. Only when the blackness of our world and the beautiful radiant whiteness of God's love are seen together do we get the picture of Christmas. I have to give you the black as the background so that you may see the picture more clearly, so it may stand out for you in finer focus and in starker detail.

So the bad news and the good news always go together, not only in the jokes we tell, but also in the gospel we believe. Hope—that's what the world must have. Hope. Despair—that's what breaks men's hearts, and hope is the heart of our Christmas.

> That night when shepherds heard the song of
> hosts angelic choiring near
> A deaf man lay in slumber's spell, and dreamed
> that he could hear.
> That night when in the cattle stall slept mother
> and child in humble fold
> A cripple turned his twisted limbs and dreamed
> that he was whole.
> That night when o'er the newborn babe a
> tender mother rose to lean,
> A loathsome leper smiled in sleep and
> dreamed that he was clean.
> That night when to the mother's breast
> the little king was held secure
> A harlot slept a happy sleep and dreamed
> that she was pure.
> That night when in a manger lay the Holy
> One who came to save
> A man turned in the sleep of death and
> dreamed there was no grave.

These are His gifts to us: hope, faith, love. What shall be our gift to Him?

> What shall I give Him, poor as I am?
> If I were a shepherd, I'd give Him a lamb.
> If I were a wiseman, I'd do my part,
> What shall I give Him?
> Give Him my heart.
>
> —Christina Rosetti

# THE UNCLAIMED GIFT
John 1:10-14

"They're bound to come and see us on Christmas Day," they said, "so we'll buy a gift for them." But Christmas Day passed, and they didn't come; so they just left the gift under the tree. All the rest had been opened and enjoyed. One lonely little package lay there under the tree, because they were sure that in just a day or two, they would be stopping by to claim their gift. It came time to take the tree down. So they just laid the little gift up in the corner, and it stayed there gathering dust. About springtime, they put it away in the closet. And there it remained, the ribbon a little bit frayed and the paper a little bit torn. The unclaimed gift.

It's the same picture that we find in the Gospel of John, chapter 1. We're familiar with the Christmas story in Luke—shepherds and angels and a baby in a manger. And we read every year the Christmas story in Matthew, Wise-men coming from afar, bringing their gifts, and then outwitting King Herod. But seldom do we read the Christmas story in the Gospel of John. The Christmas story in John is so brief in words, yet so profound in its depth and meaning. "The Word was made flesh, and dwelt among us, (and we beheld his glory, the glory as of the only begotten of the Father,) full of grace and truth." John chapter 1, verse 14, and also verse 11: "He came unto his own, and his own received him not."

You may take that as a summary of the whole life and ministry of Jesus if you like. You may take it as a kind of theme upon which all the rest of the symphony is built. "He came unto his own, and his own received him not." You pick up the theme in Bethlehem, "No room in the inn." You pick it up again in Nazareth. There was not room for Him in His home town. They took Him out to a cliff and tried to kill Him. There was not room for Him in the religious establishment. You will remember their rejection of Him. At the last, there was not room for Him on earth, and so they suspended Him above it on a cross. It's a theme that comes up again and again and again in that gospel story. "He came unto his own, and his own received him not."

The unclaimed gift. Christ himself is the gift of Christmas. And along with Christ much else that goes unclaimed. His peace goes unclaimed; His message of good news go unheard. It is broadcast through all the world, and yet men and women stop their ears that they may not hear. Not long ago on a Sunday morning, a preacher turned the corner to come into the church building, and there on the corner just across the street a man was buying a newspaper. Now the preacher surmised by the way that the man was dressed that he was not on his way to the service. And as he put that big bundle of newspaper under his arm, the preacher wanted to roll down the window and shout to him and say, "Come inside; there's good news inside." Because without looking at that paper, he knew that it was filled with bad news. Have you ever bought one that wasn't? I can tell you that tomorrow's newspaper, or the day after, or the newspaper a year from now like the newspaper today will be filled with bad news. They tried to come out with a paper that would only print the good news. They couldn't sell it. It was a business failure. While the world is going home with an arm load of bad news, we wish so much that we could give them a heart full of good news. But the good news goes unheard.

A minister said that on a Christmas Sunday morning, he was not as prepared as he usually was. He'd had a busy week; he had had a lot of demands on his time; and he was not quite as well prepared as he would like to have been, but he said as he drove to church that Sunday morning, "I'm going to preach a great sermon this morning." He said it to himself, of course, since no one else would have been likely to believe it. He said to himself, "I'm going to preach a good sermon this morning. It's Christmas, and I'm going to preach a great sermon." Then a second thought came to him. "And I'm going to preach a great sermon this morning, not because I'm so skilled at oratory, not because of my talents or gifts, but because I've got a message that can't lose."

We have the custom that when we employ a new minister, he comes to the church for an interview and is presented to the congregation through a sermon. We refer to it rather crassly as a "trial sermon." I know of a minister who went off to preach a trial sermon on Christmas Sunday, and all of his minister friends said, "He can't lose." We ministers know that you can't take a subject like that and fail. He was bound to get the call.

Why? Because of the message. Because of the best news that anybody can ever tell. With that kind of news to tell, the least-skilled orator cannot fail. And yet for many, the good news is not heard. The gift is unclaimed.

There is a power unclaimed. Imagine that you had never heard of electricity. You did not know that such a thing as electricity existed. You went to my home. I neglected to tell you about electricity. You stumble around every night in darkness, unnecessarily, because if someone had just told you about it, you could have gone over to the wall and flipped the little switch and the whole room would have been bathed in light. The potential for that light was there, was present, but you didn't know about it, and you walked in darkness.

The dynamos of God are humming. The generators of God are hard at work. Light is available for all who walk in darkness, but some do not know the switch is there; and some, knowing it, will not throw the switch. And so they walk in darkness when light is readily available. The unclaimed power.

Once the Ohio River froze over, and then as the ice was breaking up, it created a great problem. There was a great ice jam, and they were afraid that it was going to destroy some of the bridges. They thought about dynamite, but they kept putting it off, because they said, "All we really need is two or three days of good sunlight, and that will do the job." Now there is an enormous difference between dynamite and sunlight, isn't there? Dynamite makes a terrible noise, and shakes the earth with a terrible tremor; and the sun comes up without a sound, and shakes nothing on the earth, and yet the quiet, soft power of the sun, they said, is more beneficial than our dynamite. Doesn't that sound like the gospel of Christ?

Softly, quietly, reaching out to work its magic in the world. More powerful than all the booming forces of men. The power that's needed in our day is the power that Christ came to bring into the world. And it is a power that is not claimed.

Then there is the unclaimed presence. There are people living in loneliness who could have the presence in their lives every day. People are walking alone who do not need to walk alone. How sad it is to see the nature of the unclaimed gift, the peace, the power, the presence, all available to us in Christ. He is the unclaimed gift of Christmas.

But why do men not claim Him? Why do men not have that

93

presence? That peace? That power? Sometimes it is because of doubt. If you were to say to me today at the door, "Come over to my house this afternoon; I'm going to give you a million dollars," I won't be there. I don't believe you are going to give me $1,000,000. I don't even believe you have $1,000,000. And if you had it, I don't believe you'd give it to me. So if the promise were real, and if the gift were real, it would go unclaimed simply because I doubted the reality of it. How many people are there in the world, who because they will not forgive themselves, or anyone else, doubt that there is any forgiveness in the world? Since they are unforgiving with themselves, they presume that God is no better than they are, and that God cannot forgive their sins. They believe their stain is too deep, and so God's great gift of forgiveness lies there unclaimed simply because they doubted that it exists.

If you were to go to Mexico City and take the city tour, they'd take you down to that great massive cathedral that is at the heart of Mexico City. And as they were showing you the beautiful interior of that cathedral, they could point out to you the damage that was caused by a fire a few years back. The fire came about through a short circuit in the electrical wiring of an altar in that cathedral. It is rather strange to listen to the guide tell you that the fire was caused by a short circuit in the altar of forgiveness. Oh, how many short circuits I have seen in the altar of forgiveness! Sometimes people didn't know that forgiveness was available. Sometimes they heard the message, but they couldn't believe it was so. Sometimes nobody told them what response God expected them to make to His gracious offer. For one reason or another, there was a short circuit in the altar of forgiveness, and the power did not come through. So if you doubt the reality of God's promise, if you do not believe that He is who He said He was, and that He did what He came to do, then all God's rich blessings will not be yours, simply because of doubt.

It's easy to doubt. Isn't it? We remember the song, "I Heard the bells on Christmas Day, their old familiar carols play, and wild and sweet the words repeat, of peace on earth, good will to men." "Then in despair I bowed my head, there is no peace on earth, I said. For hate is strong, and mocks the song of peace on earth, good will to men."

Does it ever seem to you that life and circumstances mock

God's promises? That there is no peace to be found? That He is not a living presence in our world? That He's abandoned it and abandoned us in the process? That's a very common way to feel. But we've got to get out of that pit of doubt, and we've got to believe; believe strongly and firmly that Christ did, in fact, come into the world as God's Son and as the world's Savior, and that He reaches out to us in love today, and that He wants us to reach out to Him, too.

Sometimes it is the distractions of the world that cause us to fail to claim our gift. We know about the gift, and we believe in the gift, and we really intend to pick up our gift one of these days, but we're distracted. Our attention is drawn to other things, and so the gift goes unclaimed. Did you see in the paper that the greatest place for astronomy in the world is a mountaintop in Arizona that is in the middle of an Indian Reservation? And they've picked this place for their mighty telescopes for three reasons. One, obviously, it's on the top of a mountain. Two, it's in a part of the country that is very seldom cloudy. Third, they picked this site because it was far from any city so that the light of the stars was not competing with the man-made light of our cities. Does it seem to you, this Christmas, that the twinkling of the man-made lights of our holiday obscure the light of the star, that the star of Bethlehem, is not seen as clearly as it might be because the twinkling lights of our trivial concerns distract us and we cannot see it clearly?

Sometimes the gift is not claimed simply through neglect. We always have in our church office a shelf of unclaimed Bibles. And every two or three years, we gather up the ones whose names we do not recognize and have never been returned to the owner, and we put them to some good use. Now I don't think it's any bad commentary on our characters that we forget where we've left a Bible. It says that probably most of us have more than one Bible, and that's good isn't it? While we're using one, we're quite certain that the other will turn up, that we've only hidden it from ourselves in some place. I don't think there is anything sinister about all these unclaimed Bibles. They only serve to illustrate the fact that in every Bible, there is a gift—Christ. And He goes often unclaimed simply through neglect. Not that we doubted. Not that we were caught up in the world. We simply neglect to take the benefit that is ours through the presence of Christ in the world.

And what are the consequences? Well, we ourselves are made poorer. Can you imagine having been present at the feeding of the five thousand, and eating no bread or fish? Can you imagine yourself sitting there on the green grass looking over the blue Sea of Galilee and seeing the miracle of the loaves and fishes and saying, "I'm not going to eat any of that"? Not only would you have gone hungry physically, but you would have been the poorer spiritually because of it. Imagine yourself a shepherd sitting on a hillside one night when suddenly the heavens are opened and the angels sing. And imagine yourself closing your eyes and saying, "I'm not going to look. I'm not going to look at any angels. Why that light's so bright, it might put my eyes out." Can you imagine stopping your ears and saying, "I don't want to hear it"? Yet that is what we are sometimes doing. The sweet songs of the gospel come to us, and we stop our ears. Spiritually, we close our eyes. We are like those people Jesus talked about. He said, "Your heart has waxed gross; your ears are dull of hearing; you cannot understand." Oh, how much the poorer we are when we spiritually close our eyes and ears to the truth of God. How it wounds God. How it offends God. Both those words are necessary to describe it. He is both offended and wounded when the gift goes unclaimed.

Have you ever been down to the SPCA, the Society for the Prevention of Cruelty to Animals, and walked down the hall and looked at all those cages full of unclaimed pets? Did you ever think that here is a dog that once was a little puppy and charmed a little boy's heart? Here is a cat that was a little playful kitten that meant more to a little girl than anything she could have imagined. Not long ago, a man was going down a street and saw a big homemade sign leaning up against a street sign. And the sign said, "Lost, one gray kitten." Not very far from that sign was a very brokenhearted little child who would have claimed that kitten in a moment if it could have been found.

Do you mind if I turn this sermon upside down for a moment? We have been talking about Christ, the unclaimed gift. What would be the case if He did not claim us? What if we were caged up in that SPCA and Christ came along and said, "Never saw anything like that before. I don't know anything about that." What would it be like if He would not claim us?

Now there is never any danger that He will not claim us if we claim Him. But if, on the other hand, we reject Him, then He has no other alternative but to reject us. We leave Him no choice. If we claim Him, here is His promise: "Whosoever therefore shall confess me before men, him will I confess also before my Father which is in heaven." Oh, God wants to claim you as His son or His daughter today. Jesus wants to claim you as a brother or a sister today. The church wants to claim you as a member of the family today. I promise you that if you confess His name here, Christ will stand in the presence of God Almighty and claim you there.

# PROGRAM RESOURCES

# CHRISTMAS PAGEANTS

## CHRISTMAS AROUND THE WORLD

CHOIRS: This pageant calls for an adult choir and a junior choir, seated separately.

COSTUMING: French children wear sweaters and berets.
German children wear short pants, bright suspenders, and colorful hats with long feathers.
English carolers wear mufflers, mittens, and high top hats.
Mary, Joseph, and the shepherds, wear traditional costuming, with long robes, sashes, turbans, and beards.
Candlelighters wear white capes with large bows, and light candles from a lighted one which they hold.

ENTRANCES: All participants enter from rear of auditorium, using the center aisle (except candlelighters, who use side aisles, and carolers, who enter from side of platform.) All exit to the side of the platform, return from this place for the closing circle, and then orderly exit at front after benediction.

**NARRATOR:** "For God so loved the world, that He gave His only begotten Son, that whosoever believeth in Him should not perish, but have everlasting life." Every word in this great text is significant, but of special significance is the word *world*. "For God so loved the *world*." Sometimes we here in America act as if Christmas belonged to us—as if it were an American holiday. We forget that our customs have come to us from other lands, and that it was very far away that Christ was born. Some of the customs you will hear about tonight may seem strange to you, but they are as beloved by the people of other lands as our own customs are beloved by us. You may be surprised to discover how many of our own traditions have been borrowed from the people of other nations. Come with us tonight as we listen to the beautiful carols and view the inspiring customs of "Christmas Around the World."

*(Organist begins playing softly "The First Noel.")*

**NARRATOR:** In France, we find the custom of making a Christmas scene. Each home has its homemade creche, which is the center of its decorations. The churches have ornate and elaborately lighted nativity scenes, which are the center of their services on Christmas Eve. Tonight the people of France will be singing the beautiful carol, "The First Noel."

*(As the choir sings "The First Noel," children come in carrying manger and doll and prepare the nativity scene, then leave.)*

**NARRATOR:** Another carol, unfamiliar to us but beloved by them, tells of a mother asking her daughter to come with her to see the baby Jesus.

*(Junior choir sings "Bring a Torch, Jeannete Isabella.)*

**NARRATOR:** In the Ukraine tonight, the songs of joy will not be heard. The Christmas bells will not ring out over the fertile farmlands, calling the worshipers to praise the Son of God. The iron curtain has fallen, and the dictators have decreed that there is no God. We can be certain, though, that many there will be remembering Christmases of long ago, and, though tongues and bells are silenced, in their hearts they will be praising God. Perhaps they will even secretly teach their children this old Ukranian song, "The Bell Carol."

*(Choir sings "Ukranian Bell Carol," also called "Ring, Silver Bells.")*

**NARRATOR:** In Ireland, we find the custom of candle-lighting. Every home has a lighted candle in the window, and the door is left open to signify that there is room in this home for the Lord Jesus.

*(As Junior Choir sings "Room in My Heart, Lord Jesus," children enter and light candles previously placed in the windows and on the platform.)*

**NARRATOR:** The Czechoslovakian people usher in Christmas with the ending of all quarrels. Friend and foe are visited and misunderstandings are settled. It would not be proper, they feel, to celebrate the birthday of the Prince of Peace if there were no peace in the hearts of His children. This feeling is echoed in the words of the lovely carol "I Heard the Bells on Christmas Day."

*(Soloist sings "I Heard the Bells on Christmas Day.")*

**NARRATOR:** Germany has given us many of the customs we now call our own. One that has a permanent place in our culture is the Christmas tree, and the very meaningful Christmas tree carol, "O Tannenbaum."

*(As Junior Choir sings "O Christmas Tree," children enter with a small tree on a stand, which they place on the platform and decorate, then leave.)*

**NARRATOR:** We are indebted to Germany also for probably the best-loved and most-sung Christmas carol, "Silent Night."

*(Choir sings "Silent Night.")*

**NARRATOR:** In England, we find the custom of caroling, visiting the sick and lonely to spread Christmas cheer. Listen to England's most often sung carol.

*(Men in Choir sing "God Rest Ye Merry, Gentlemen" as children dressed as carolers, with mufflers, mittens, and songbooks enter, pose as if caroling, and then leave on final verse.)*

**NARRATOR:** Here in America, a most important part of Christmas is the acting out of the story of Jesus' birth. All over our land, children in churches and schools are doing as these children are tonight.

*(As Choir sings "It Came Upon the Midnight Clear," children dressed as Mary and Joseph enter and take places at manger left by earlier group. Shepherds then enter and kneel at manger. On the final verse, all leave.)*

**NARRATOR:** Our country is one of great variety. Our people have different ancestries, different customs, and different ways to express their universal joy over the birth of Christ. Because of the great suffering of the American Negro, his music is especially touching and, at Christmas, especially joyous. Here is an old spiritual that seems to throb with the very pulse beat of life, "Rise Up, Shepherds, and Foller."

*(Choir sings "Rise Up, Shepherds, and Foller.")*

**NARRATOR:** Many of England's early colonists settled in the land-locked valleys of the Appalachian mountains. Here they preserved much of the speech and many of the songs of old England. Often, they added a touch of their own that seems to make these songs ring with the haunting echoes of the mountains. Listen to this stirring ballad,

*(Soloist sings "I Wonder As I Wander.")*

**NARRATOR:** Next the choir will sing for us a few of the beloved American carols. You may feel free to join in and sing along with them, or to sit and listen.

*(Any number of familiar carols may be inserted here, such as "O Little Town of Bethlehem" and "O Come, All Ye Faithful." After the last carol, as the organist plays softly, all the children enter and join hands in a circle.)*

**NARRATOR:** As these children have joined hands, so our customs have joined together the people of many lands and languages, and the warmth of Christmas has melted the barrier between us, that there may indeed be peace on earth, good will among men. And the farther we spread the good tidings of Christmas, the more men will crave peace and understanding. Then the possibility of a world of safety and happiness will become a reality. "For God sent not His Son into the world to condemn the world, but that the world, through Him, might be saved." Join with us, as we stand and sing together, "Joy to the World."

**BENEDICTION**

# THE STORY OF JESUS

On one side of the platform are a rocking chair, a low stool, and an end table with a lamp. On the opposite side is a manger with hay and a doll. Children play the parts of Joseph, Mary, shepherds, and the Wise-men.

As the play opens, the choir has already assembled and the lights are all turned out.

When the lights come on, Mother is seated, rocking and sewing.

**CHOIR:** Chorus of "Tell Me the Story of Jesus" (As the chorus ends, girl enters, dressed in long nightgown and nightcap.)

**GIRL:** Mother, I'm ready for bed now. Would you please tell me a story?

**MOTHER:** All right, you sit here beside me, and I'll tell you one of the most wonderful stories ever written. It was many, many years ago in a land far away that God told a Jewish girl named Mary that she had been chosen to be the mother of His Son. Mary and Joseph, her husband, lived in Nazareth, but the king of the land said that all the people must go to their hometown to sign their names and be taxed. Since they belonged to the house of David, and Bethlehem was the city of David, they had to go to Bethlehem.

Mary rode a little donkey, and Joseph walked by her side. It was a long journey. There were hills to climb and rough roads to walk over. It was very late when at last they saw the lights of Bethlehem twinkling before them.

**CHOIR:** Sing "O Little Town of Bethlehem." (Mary and Joseph enter and walk down the aisle. Mary sits and Joseph stands beside her.)

**MOTHER:** The city was crowded; the streets were full of others who had come to obey the king. Joseph found the inn and knocked on the door. "No room," said the innkeeper. "No

105

room, I'm sorry." He looked at Mary, and she looked so tired. "I have a nice clean stable with fresh hay. You could stay there if you like." Mary smiled her thanks and Joseph led her to the stable. It was cozy and warm, and they were very grateful for the shelter.

It was very quiet in Bethlehem. Everyone was sleeping. It was at this time that God chose to keep His promise to Mary and cause her to give birth to His son. It was quiet—a silent night.

**CHOIR:** Sing "Silent Night." *(At the close of the song, shepherds enter right.)*

**MOTHER:** Out in the hills, the shepherds were watching over their sheep. It was still on the hillside, too. The soft baaing of the lambs was all that could be heard. Suddenly a great light shone from the sky and an angel appeared. *(Angel enters right.)* The shepherds were frightened, but the angel said, "I've come to bring you good news. Tonight in the city of David the Savior, Christ the Lord, is born. You'll find Him wrapped in swaddling clothes, lying in a manger." Then other angels appeared, and they said, "Glory to God in the highest, and on earth, peace toward men of good will."

**CHOIR:** Sing "While Shepherds Watched Their Flocks."

**MOTHER:** After the angels left, the shepherds went at once to the stable, where they knelt and worshiped the baby. They left very quietly, for their hearts were full of joy and wonder. They were amazed that God had allowed them to be among the first to welcome His Son to earth.

**CHOIR:** Another verse of "While Shepherds Watched Their Flocks" *(as shepherds exit down the middle aisle.)*

**MOTHER:** In a land far away from Bethlehem, there were Wise-men who studied the stars. One night they saw a bright and glorious star. They knew it was to announce the birth of a very special king. They loaded their camels with beautiful gifts and started out to find the king. They went through small villages, large cities, and barren deserts, always following the glorious star. At last they came to Jerusalem. They went to King Herod and asked where the baby, King of the Jews, was to be born. The teachers in the palace told them that God's Word said the baby would be born in Bethlehem. "Come back and tell me where the baby is so that I can worship him too," the king said.

The Wise-men hurried to Bethlehem, and there the star stopped over the house where Mary, Joseph, and the baby were. They knelt and gave the baby Jesus gifts of gold, frankincense, and myrrh.

**CHOIR:** Sing the last verse of "The First Noel." *(Wise-men enter and kneel, offering gifts.)*

**MOTHER:** God sent an angel to the Wise-men and warned them that the king wished to harm the baby, not to worship Him. So they must not go back to the palace in Jerusalem. The Wise-men, like the shepherds, were filled with joy and wonder as they left the baby and went home another way.

**CHOIR:** Sing the last verse of "We Three Kings."

**Girl:** *(stands)* Mother, did the king hurt the baby?

**MOTHER:** Oh no *(takes child in arms)*. An angel came to Joseph, too, and told him that the king was afraid Jesus would grow up and take his throne from him, and they must leave Bethlehem quickly and stay away until God told them it was safe for them again. Mary and Joseph took the baby to Egypt and stayed till the wicked king died. *(Child goes to sleep.)*

**CHOIR:** Sing last verse of "Silent Night." *(Mary and Joseph exit center aisle as choir sings.)*

**MOTHER:** Mary and Joseph never forgot the things that happened in Bethlehem. They remembered the shepherds' visit and the Wise-men with their glorious gifts. Our Bible tells us Mary kept all these things and cherished them in her heart.

**MOTHER:** *(Sings "Sleep, My Child"; then exits, carrying child.)*

# THE CAROLS OF CHRISTMAS

This simple program is easily produced. A narrator tells the story of the origin of each carol, and it is then sung either by the congregation, by a soloist, or by a group. The program is best received if the songs are sung by a variety of singers.

### SILENT NIGHT

Mice had eaten the bellows of the church organ at Arnsdorf, Austria. So Joseph Mohr, the parish priest, wrote the words to a new song, and Franz Gruber, the schoolmaster and church organist, wrote the music so that the song could be accompanied by a guitar. Interestingly, Joseph Mohr was sent from one poor parish to another and died in obscurity. Gruber also died before the song became well known.

### O COME ALL YE FAITHFUL

This lovely hymn was written by an unknown composer in France early in the eighteenth century. When first published in 1751, it was published in Latin. Over forty different English translations of the hymn have been made.

### O LITTLE TOWN OF BETHLEHEM

The beloved Boston pastor, Phillips Brooks, wanted to do something different for his children's Christmas program at the church. Three years before, he had been in Bethlehem on Christmas Eve. Thinking back upon that night, he wrote the words, and the church organist, Lewis Redner, wrote the melody, for "O Little Town of Bethlehem."

### HARK, THE HERALD ANGELS SING

Prolific hymn writer Charles Wesley gave us this song. Originally, the first line read, "Hark, how all the welkin rings." *Welkin* is an old English word for the heavens or the sky. Fourteen years later, Wesley changed the line to "Hark, the herald angels sing." Wesley got the idea for the song one Christmas morning as he walked to church, listening to the bells in the distance.

## WHILE SHEPHERDS WATCHED THEIR FLOCKS BY NIGHT

William Gardiner was a stocking manufacturer in Leicester, England. He had an exceptional knowledge of music. He took the melodies of Haydn, Mozart, and Beethoven and adapted to them English poems to create churchly hymns. In this way, people learned an appreciation for the music of the master composers. He took Nahum Tate's poem and a tune by Beethoven and married them to create this lovely carol.

## THE FIRST NOEL

This is a true folk song, a ballad originated by an unknown author and sung among the common people. The word *noel* means "carol" but has also come to mean Christmas. People have been singing carols since A.D. 129, but none has been more beloved than this by an unknown writer.

## I WONDER AS I WANDER

John Jacob Niles is a collector of folk songs and mountain ballads. In a southern Appalachian town, an itinerant evangelist set up his tent on the courthouse lawn and hung his wash from the Confederate monument. Niles went that night and heard a fourteen-year-old girl sing the first stanza of this hymn. He asked her where she had learned it. She couldn't remember. He asked if there were more to the song. There wasn't. The next day, the evangelist left town, and Niles never saw him or his family again. Adding additional verses, John Jacob Niles published this lovely American carol.

## GOD REST YE MERRY, GENTLEMEN

This is perhaps the favorite old English carol with a tune as old as itself and known to nearly everyone. Often sung in the open air like the first great Christmas carol sung in Judea, this tune in particular was a favorite of strolling bands of minstrels and groups of little children, going from door to door in the streets and highways of old England. From that day to this, this song has expressed the joy and hope of the Christmas season.

## ANGELS FROM THE REALMS OF GLORY

Written by James Montgomery, this hymn was first printed December 24, 1816, in a paper he edited. Included in one of the first hymnbooks used in the Church of England, it had a wide circulation in both England and America. Formerly it was sung to the melody of an old French carol. Now it appears with music by Henry Smart.

### IT CAME UPON THE MIDNIGHT CLEAR
A Unitarian minister in Boston, Edmund H. Sears, wrote a poem in 1849, and a year later, Richard S. Willis wrote this joyful music for it, giving us one of the few hymns of the nineteenth century with the real Christmas message, "Peace on earth, good will towards men."

### WHAT CHILD IS THIS?
The words of this carol are sung to the old English tune "Greensleeves," which was popular before the time of Queen Elizabeth I. It was one of the best-liked tunes of its day, and Shakespeare mentions it twice in "The Merry Wives of Windsor." The present words about the Christ Child were written by William C. Dix during the reign of Queen Elizabeth I.

### AWAY IN A MANGER
This simple hymn, beloved by children everywhere, is often called "Luther's Cradle Hymn." Some say Luther did not write it, but that some artist imagined he would choose this type of song to sing his own child to sleep. Regardless of origin, it is one of our favorite Christmas songs.

### JOY TO THE WORLD
This inspiring carol was written by Isaac Watts, the founder of English hymn writing. It was first published in 1719. The music is usually attributed to George Frederick Handel.

### WE THREE KINGS OF ORIENT ARE
This is a carol particularly associated with Twelfth Night, celebrated in most countries as the day the three Wise-men from the East were led to Bethlehem. The words and music were written in the year 1857 by John Hopkins. In it, each of the kings of the Orient tells what gifts he has brought to the Christ Child.

# CHRISTMAS PROMOTIONS

**Birthday Party**

Secure a worker and a birthday card for each ten people you wish to see in attendance. Ask the worker to get ten, including himself, to sign his birthday card indicating they will be present to wish Jesus a "Happy Birthday" on Christmas Sunday.

**Nazareth to Bethlehem**

Take the miles from Nazareth to Bethlehem (70) and divide by your desired cumulative attendance for the four Sundays of December leading up to Christmas. Each week, your attendance will determine how far you've traveled—going one fourth of the distance each time you have the desired attendance. Make a map-like chart to show progress as the whole church journeys from Nazareth to Bethlehem. Thus, if you wish to average 500 in attendance, you need a cumulative total of 2,000, and each person in attendance represents .035 miles traveled.

**Bethlehem to Egypt**

For a post-Christmas promotion, use the same idea, but journey with Jesus from Bethlehem to safety in Egypt.

**Congregational Christmas Card**

Some congregations put up a very large Christmas Card in the lobby. Members sign their names there and instead of sending cards to each other, contribute to the church the amount they would have spent for these cards and postage.

**Light the Candles**

Large posters of candles can dramatize attendance or offering goals for each December Sunday with the "flame" added when the goal is reached. Or a large wreath with missing parts can be used in the same way.

## Leftover Dinner

One congregation has a great "leftover dinner" a day or two after Christmas. Each family brings its leftover food, and they put it all together for a post-holiday meal. It's a grand way to promote fellowship and friendship, and it's very easy to do.

## Living Manger Scene

As a special promotion for your church in the community, you could sponsor a Living Manger Scene. Church members could take different shifts protraying Mary, Joseph, the shepherds, and the Wise-men. A more ambitious project would be a Living Christmas Tableau featuring live depictions of various Christmas scenes. Narration could be printed, or you could use guides to tell the story. An electronics wizard might be able to set up music and narration on tapes.

If you have found this book helpful, you might also appreciate *Celebrating the Resurrection* (#3021) by the same authors.